What's Your Weirdest Case?

Judges Answer Questions On The Courts

The cartoon on the cover was created by Griffin Haz, a winner of the First Amendment Cartoon Contest for K-12 students. The contest is sponsored by the Administrative Office of the Courts, in partnership with the Constitutional Rights Foundation and the California State PTA, to increase student understanding of the Bill of Rights and the United States Constitution. Winners are announced on Law Day, a national day to celebrate the rule of law and its contributions to the freedoms Americans enjoy, as well as the essential role informed citizens play in a democracy. To view other winning cartoons, and for more information about the contest visit: **www.courtsed.org**

Table of Contents

Introduction..4

Section I...9

   Juries..11

   Trials..14

   Being A Judge...30

   Lawyers...43

   Prisoners...49

   Sentencing...52

   Prison..54

Section II..57

   Constitutional Rights.....................................58

   What Do Lawyers Do?....................................65

   How Judges Become Judges...........................70

   Jury Service...75

   Who *Are* Those People In The Courtroom?...........80

   What is a Trial?...85

   Evidence: The Role of Judges & Juries............90

   Sentencing...94

   Alternative Dispute Resolution.......................98

   Appeals...103

   The Juvenile Delinquency System, Simply
      Described...108

   What Happens In Family Court?.....................111

Appendix (state courts) 118

Appendix (federal courts).......................................119

Introduction

Every year our Court hosts classes from our local schools. Children from many different grades, and from both public and private schools, tour our courthouses. They watch trials, but of course they see only a small, fragmentary portion of the case, and so it is difficult to know what it is, exactly, one is seeing. The classes do meet with a Judge and ask questions, but there is never enough time to talk about all the issues the children, their teachers, and accompanying parents, may have.

This collection was assembled to address some of those limitations. In section I of this pamphlet, I have collected a series of questions from visiting schools, and asked our Judges to answer them. There are great questions here, and odd ones, funny questions and serious ones; and some which were difficult to answer. But we did not change any of them. We did our best to answer each one because these were, after all, what the children wanted to know.

My thanks to these Judges of my Court for their tireless work on this project: Kay Tsenin, Monica Wiley, Loretta Giorgi, Linda Colfax, Jeff Ross, Gail Dekreon, Anne-Christine Massullo, Marla Miller, Andrew Cheng, Susan Breall, Angela Bradstreet, and Suzanne Bolanos.

✧

I have also included in section II a series of columns I wrote for the California Council for the Social Studies Newsletter as my column "Just Comment"< http://www.ccss.org/>, as well as guest columns by Judges Patrick Mahoney, Monica F. Wiley and Commissioner Rebecca L. Wightman. These items address, in perhaps a more systematic way, issues essential to a basic understanding of how our courts work. These columns may not be suitable for the lower grades. But teachers might find them useful as they seek to augment their curricula and integrate an understanding about the courts into other course work, such as that in English, Social Studies, and History.

☼

I and my colleagues on the Superior Court look forward to working ever more closely with our schools in an effort to ensure that the citizens, and future voters and leaders of the state of California, have a good understanding of the critical role our courts play in the guarantees of a free, open, and democratic society. If we do not understand how our courts work, we will not be able to protect them; and without effective, independent courts, the promises of the Constitution are nothing but faint words on old paper. Every generation must learn anew the genius that is the American system of government, including the crucial role of the third branch of government—the courts—where rights are guaranteed, disputes resolved, and the law is enforced.

Curtis E.A. Karnow
Judge Of The Superior Court, County of San Francisco

November, 2012

Calaveras County Courthouse
Completed 1850
Local history has it that the county seat was "captured" from
Double Springs, a cattle ranch-cum-mining town, when residents
of nearby Jackson invited county officials for a few rounds of
drinks and then made off with the county records. The remains of
this building, made of camphor panels shipped from China, can
still be seen in Double Springs, making it one of the oldest
surviving structures once used as a courthouse in California.
Courtesy Calaveras County Historical Society

*In California, trials have been held in all sorts of courthouses,
from ramshackle wooden structures ...*

Humboldt County Courthouse
Completed 1889
Thirteen zinc statues adorned the perimeter of the roof and the tower of this grand Italianate building in Eureka. Minerva, the Roman goddess of wisdom, was placed at the top of the tower, surrounded by four statues of Justice and others representing Flora, Ceres, Fortuna, and Juno. Minerva tilted in the 1906 earthquake, after which the statues were removed. The courthouse survived a fire in 1924, but another quake in 1954 cracked the building and the courthouse was vacated. In 1956, the condemned courthouse was demolished to make room for a more modern facility.
Courtesy Humboldt County Historical Society

... to the most elegant temples of Justice. Other photographs are available at http://www.courts.ca.gov/4563.htm

Section I

Questions From the Kids

Juries

What is jury duty?

Jury Duty is the obligation we all have as citizens to respond when we are called to serve on a jury. In most cases, it is the jury which decides who wins and who loses a case filed in court. For some people, jury duty lasts a day or two, as they participate in jury selection. For those who are finally selected to be on the jury, their duty might last a total of three or four days, a week to two weeks, or longer, depending on how long the trial lasts.

Citizens usually find out they have been called for jury duty when they get a notice in the mail. The notice tells them to come to the courthouse on a specific date, to be ready to serve on a jury.

Who qualifies to serve for duty?

Anyone over the age of 18 who is a citizen of the United States, is mentally competent, can understand and speak English and has not been found guilty of a felony (a crime that can be punished by a sentence of more than a year in state prison) and who is a resident of the county in which the court house is located.

What is the role of jurors?

Jurors listen to the evidence, such as testimony of witnesses. They review evidence such as photographs, documents, diagrams and sometimes other items that a party presents (and a Judge allows). From that evidence, the jurors decide what they believe are the facts, because often the facts are in dispute.

Jurors have to evaluate the evidence and observe the witnesses. Once the jurors decide what the facts are, then they apply the law as told to them by the Judge to determine the verdict. In criminal case the verdict is "Guilty" or "Not Guilty." In civil cases the jury decides if any harm was committed, who committed the harm, and how much money (damages) to award the party who was harmed.

Why can't jurors talk during trials?

Noise and talking during trial disturbs other jurors who are trying to pay careful attention to the testimony. Even when there is a break in the proceedings, the jurors cannot talk *about the case* with anyone until the case is over, that is, until after all the evidence has been presented, the Judge instructs them on the law, and then only when all 12 of the jurors are present in the jury room. Early discussions might lead the jury to decide the case before they have actually seen all the evidence, and before the jury even knows the law they need to apply.

How do you get chosen for jury duty?

In San Francisco we obtain names from the records from the Department of Motor Vehicles, and voter registration documents. When you are called for jury duty, you will be sent to a court room. There, you will answer questions from the Judge and lawyers. You may be excused if it looks like the specific case is one in which it would be very hard for you to be fair. For example, if the case is about a stolen car, and you just had your car stolen, you might find it difficult to be fair to both sides. If so, the Judge will excuse you. The lawyers, too, can excuse a certain number of people, without giving a reason. We allow this to make sure that both sides in a trial have an important role in shaping the jury that will decide their fate.

Does work pay you if you have to go to jury duty?

Some employers do pay, and some do not. All government agencies pay people for jury duty, for however long someone is on the jury. Some employers only pay for a few days, or a week, and some don't pay at all. Jurors get paid by the State but not much, about $16.50 a day....barely enough for parking and a hot dog.

How often do you get called for jury duty?

It varies. These days it is about once every two years. The time period is different in different counties.

What about juries for murder trials?

There is very little difference between a jury for a murder trial or a jury for anything else except that attorneys get more challenges (the right to excuse more jurors).

Who leads the jury members and speaks for them?

The jurors elect a foreperson or "presiding juror." The presiding juror makes sure everyone has a chance to be heard, and makes sure the jury deliberations are conducted in a orderly way.

What about celebrities and jury duty?

Almost everyone has the right and obligation to serve on a jury if they are qualified. Celebrities, mayors, star athletes--and even Judges--serve along with everyone else on juries.

Trials

Why do some trials go on for months?

Most trials do not last long, and take from between three days to two weeks to complete. However, there are some cases that involve very complicated factual and legal issues. These trials can take several weeks to several months to complete. These longer cases often have many pre-trial motions to be heard by the Judge (before the jury is picked), and which may require testimony of witnesses. Jury selection may also be very complicated and lengthy if the issues in the case involve a subject about which people have strong feelings and beliefs, because that may make it difficult to find jurors who will be impartial and unbiased (for example, a death penalty case.) The case may also require the testimony of a lot of witnesses, and may require the jury to review a lot of documents. Finally, some jurors just take a considerable amount of time to think about a case and come to a decision.

Can a witness for the defense object to something the plaintiff says?

Witnesses are not allowed to object to questions asked, or to answers given. Only the plaintiff's or defendant's attorneys, or people who are acting as their own attorney (or in some situations, the Judge) are allowed to object to questions. Lawyers, and people who are acting as their own lawyer, can also ask that improper testimony be stricken from the record. Witnesses are only allowed to give their testimony under oath. They must answer the question unless the Judge says they do not have to do so.

Why do cases get postponed and how come they are postponed for so long?

A case may get postponed for a variety of reasons. For example, a party or witness might not be available on the date that was previously set, or on the date that the lawyer previously chose. A lawyer might be involved in different (perhaps long) trial. Sometimes additional pre-trial discovery (that is, exchanges of information or documents or taking of depositions, i.e., statements of witnesses) may be necessary. Sometimes, we do not have courtrooms available to hear the matter, due to a backlog of cases in the court system.

What is the basis for sustaining or overruling something?

A Judge *sustains* or *overrules* objections to questions directed at witnesses or to the admission of evidence (e.g., documents or items related to the case).   If the Judge sustains the objection, the witness will not answer. If the objection is overruled, the witness will answer.

Evidence (such as witness testimony, or a document) is admitted or excluded by the Judge based upon certain laws, called the rules of evidence. There are many of these rules. For example, one rule is called the *hearsay* rule. Under that rule, a witness in court cannot recite what someone *else* told him. We have this rule because there is no way to cross-examine the other person to see if she was really telling the truth or not when she spoke to the witness. So a Judge might sustain a hearsay objection if the witness was asked something like, "What did Elaine tell you about the car accident?" This might be hearsay, because Elaine is not in court to be cross-examined, and we can't be sure she was telling the truth, or exactly what she meant when she was talking about the car accident.

Why do lawyers question witnesses' backgrounds?

Because part of the jury or Judge's job is to determine whether a witness is giving truthful or believable testimony, it is important for a lawyer to give the jury a sense of who the witness is. This is particularly true with those we call "expert witnesses" who are allowed to give opinions on matters such as the physical condition of an injured person, or the results of a scientific test, or whether one party was acting appropriately under the circumstances of the case. Asking witnesses to give information about their backgrounds (what do they do for a living, their education, training and experience, how long they have been doing what they do) helps the jury or Judge determine how much weight they will give to each witness' testimony. Sometimes witnesses may be asked questions about their background to show that perhaps the jury or Judge should not give their testimony any weight. For example, if a witness has been convicted of a crime (e.g. theft or fraud), that might tend to show that the witness is not a truthful person.

How many times can a person appeal a case?

As a general rule, a case can be appealed once to the next highest court. In cases heard in the Superior Court (where most trials are held), the appeal goes to the Court of Appeal. That court, after hearing the appeal, can uphold the decision of the Superior Court or overturn the case. If it overturns the verdict or decision of the Superior Court, the Court of Appeal may send it back to the lower court with instructions to do something specific with the case or to be reheard, or can reverse the decision without a further hearing. The party who lost in the Court of Appeal can try to have the California Supreme Court take the case. The Supreme Court rarely agrees to hear such appeals. If the state Supreme Court does take the case, it can then issue a ruling either upholding the decision of the Court of Appeal, or reversing with instructions on what should happen next in the case.

In some cases which involve a *federal* (as opposed to state) legal issue, the party losing in the state Supreme Court can then ask the United States Supreme Court (in Washington D.C.) to hear the case. Here, too, the U.S. Supreme Court very rarely agrees to hear cases.

How does the jury come up with a verdict?

A jury, after hearing the evidence presented in a case, is given "instructions" by the Judge on the law that they must apply. These instructions are given orally by the Judge and copies of the instructions are provided to the jury. Then the jury is sent into a jury deliberation room where they talk about the case, review the evidence presented and apply the facts they deem to have been proven to the law given to them by the Judge. They then try to come to a decision (called a verdict). In a criminal case, all twelve jurors must agree on the verdict. In a civil case, 9 of the twelve jurors must agree on the verdict. If they are having difficulty agreeing on a verdict they can ask that the Court Reporter read back witness testimony. They can also ask the Judge to clarify the instructions if they need further guidance. Hopefully this will help them to reach a verdict. If, after making a concerted effort, the jury cannot reach a verdict, the court declares a mistrial and the case must be retried.

What is the role of the court and who are the people that work there?

The Court system is a separate branch of our government and is charged with resolving legal disputes and interpreting the laws of our state and country. Judges do this without consideration of personal beliefs, biases, prejudices or politics. In the state of California we have the Superior Court, also known as the trial court. Each county has Judges of the Superior Court assigned to hear cases arising within that county. The next level is the Court of Appeal which hears appeals from cases heard in the Superior Court. Then we have the California Supreme Court which may hear appeals from decisions of the Court of Appeal.

At the trial court level, each Judge sits in a courtroom that will hear either civil cases (private civil disputes), criminal cases, juvenile cases (cases involving children accused of committing crimes or cases where a child has been removed from his home because he has been abused or neglected by a parent or guardian), or family court cases (divorce and child custody dispute cases). The Judge hears each case, determines how each case will proceed and be conducted, and determines the law that applies in each case. Either the Judge or a jury resolves the factual issues that are presented by the parties.

Each courtroom has a court clerk who is responsible for keeping written notes (called minutes) of what occurred in each case, keeping track of evidence presented in a trial, assisting jurors, attorneys, and litigants communicate with the court, and keeping the business of the court organized for the Judge. Some courtrooms also have a court reporter assigned to take down everything that is said at a hearing or in a trial. The court reporter transcribes the record of the proceeding into a written transcript for the court, Judge and parties, if it is needed. Other courts may have the proceeding mechanically recorded, such as with a tape or digital recorder. Some courtrooms have a bailiff assigned to keep the courtroom secure and safe. Bailiffs make sure that disruptive persons are removed from court, and they transport persons who are in custody (in jail) to and from the courthouse. Bailiffs are also known as deputy sheriffs.

Explain Plaintiff versus Defendant.

The Plaintiff in a case is the one who files the action or lawsuit. In criminal cases, the plaintiff is the District Attorney or State Attorney General on behalf of the People of the State of California. In a civil case, the plaintiff can be an individual, a corporation or agency, or a governmental entity.

In a civil case, the defendant is the person who is being sued by the Plaintiff. Again, a defendant can be a person, a corporation or agency or a governmental entity. In a criminal case, the defendant is the person or company that is accused of committing a crime.

Plaintiffs and defendants are sometimes together referred to as the "parties" or the "litigants".

Why is everyone suing each other?

The courts are the place that parties go to redress civil or criminal wrongs, to have laws interpreted, to obtain justice, and to resolve disputes. Society encourages people to have their disputes resolved in an orderly civilized manner, in court, and not to seek out their own retribution or judgments outside the confines of the law. That is why it seems that there are a lot of cases. There is a constant need to resolve disputes or interpret our laws, because our society (and the issues affecting it) change and evolve.

Most of the cases in our courts have real issues that need to be resolved. However, in some rare instances there are some people who see the court process as a way to harass or annoy other parties, and they file endless numbers of lawsuits for the sole purpose of annoying people and have them spend endless hours and money defending these suits. In response to this problem, the legislature has passed laws that allow the Courts to declare these persons as *vexatious litigants* and set up special procedures to ensure that they do not abuse the court process.

Have you seen many cases involving corporations?

Yes, a corporation generally has the same rights and obligations as individuals and may sue and be sued.

What is the defendant Judged on?

If it is a criminal case, then the defendant is Judged on the issue of whether or not he or she is guilty of a crime.

In civil cases, the defendant may be accused of, for example, causing an accident, or breaking a promise, or not paying money he owes, or not paying child support. Civil cases are also brought to decide issues concerning divorces, such as how to divide the property owned by the family.

Whatever the type of case, a Judge or a jury has to decide based on the evidence that is presented in court. The job of the Judge who hears a case or the jury that hears a case is to: (1) determine what the true facts are based only on the evidence in court; (2) apply the law to those facts; (3) decide the case.

What are the most common issues covered in a civil courthouse?

Many cases involve landlord tenant disputes; employment claims where an employee claims that he or she was discriminated against, illegally harassed or not paid his or her proper wages and other earnings; claims that a product is defective and caused injuries; and claims that an agreement between the parties has been broken.

How is the courthouse on McAllister Street different from the one on Bryant Street?

The courthouse at 400 McAllister Street is called the "Civic Center Courthouse" because it is located in the Civic Center part of San Francisco. That building has only court functions in it, such as Judges, clerks, files, courtrooms, and Judges' chambers. Almost all of the cases in the McAllister Street court house are civil cases. Civil lawsuits concern divorce, child support, accidents, broken promises, failure to pay money, and others cases that do not involve crimes.

The courthouse at 850 Bryant Street only has criminal cases, from traffic ticket cases to misdemeanors to felonies. It is called the "Hall of Justice" because it houses various types of businesses that are related to criminal law, as well as courtrooms and Judges' chambers.

The Hall of Justice has these other offices, as well: (1) the San Francisco Police Department's Northern Police Station, Chief of Police's office and the Assistant Chiefs' offices; (2) the Sheriff Department's offices and three jails; (3) the Probation Department offices (probation officers supervise people who are convicted of a crime but are not in jail, and make sure convicted defendants do what the Judge ordered them to do); and (4) the District Attorney's office (they prosecute crimes).

The Public Defender used to have its office in the Hall of Justice, but now that office is in a new building about half a block away.

All of these other offices are called "justice partners" because they all work with criminal law and often have to work together.

Why might Judges and attorneys excuse themselves during a trial and go talk behind closed doors?

Sometimes the attorneys want to talk about something that the jury is not supposed to hear because the law does not allow it. Sometimes one of the lawyers needs to ask the Judge's permission to talk about an issue in front of the jury. Often, the lawyers have a legal dispute, such as the meaning and effect of a rule of evidence, which is for the Judge, and not the jury, to decide. Those discussions too will be held away from the jury. These private discussions may be held outside the courtroom, or sometimes the jury is excused briefly from the courtroom. Sometimes these discussions are held at 'side bar' that is, at the Judge's bench, out of the hearing of the jury.

How often do cases get to the Supreme Court?

For the United States Supreme Court there is no specific number of cases accepted each year. The Court typically hears between 60-75 oral arguments per year, and reviews approximately another 50-60 more cases on paper. The total represents a mere 1-2% of the cases submitted to the Supreme Court, which decides which cases it wants to hear.

The California Supreme Court at a typical weekly conference considers from 120 to 180 matters, primarily petitions for review and original proceedings. Many of the cases accepted by the Court at its weekly conferences will be argued orally before the full Court and will be decided by a full written opinion. The California Supreme Court usually issues just under 100 full opinions deciding cases per year. As with the United States Supreme Court, very few of the petitions for a hearing will be granted.

For both the United States Supreme Court and the California Supreme Court, the Court's refusal to grant a petition for review does not mean the supreme court agrees with the decision of the lower court. It just means the supreme court will not review it, and expresses no opinion.

How often do famous people get taken to court?

We usually do not know a famous person has been taken to court unless the news people report it in newspapers, magazines, on TV or on the internet.

Whenever a civil lawsuit or a criminal case is filed in court, whether it involves a famous person or not, a public record is made. That means anyone in the world can go to the courthouse, go in the clerk's office, check the list of every case that has been filed, and look at the file.

How do high profile people like celebrities handle private legal matters?

All claims that are filed in court are, with very few exceptions, kept in a public record so once litigation starts it is no longer private. Therefore anyone trying to keep the dispute out of the public eye may try informally to settle the matter before any court filing. Even then, leaks can occur.

Some people and companies decide not to use the courts to decide their disputes, and instead use private mediation and arbitration services. Professional mediators and arbitrators can have private sessions in an office. However, *all* parties to a case must agree before a dispute can be handled privately in this way.

What are the consequences of lying under oath?

The consequences of lying under oath can be very serious and may result in perjury or obstruction of justice charges being brought in a criminal court. A Judge also has the discretion to find the witness in contempt of court which may result in jail time.

How realistic are trials on TV like Law and Order compared with real life?

I have often seen the attorneys in a criminal case explain to the jury that the case is not going to be like the cases they see on Law and Order. Many criminal trials do not involve evidence like the high technology scientific evidence we see on shows like CSI. Instead, they just come down to whom the jury believes. The examinations of witnesses on TV often consist of objectionable questions that would not be allowed by the Judge in a real trial. Some witnesses can be on the stand for hours and even days, rather than the few second snippets that are shown on TV.

How does a case where someone is getting sued work?

I would like to start by saying that the person being sued, that is the defendant, should, in most cases, get an attorney. There are organizations that will represent a low income defendant for free or for a reduced fee. Various court pleadings must be filed by both sides. Both sides can examine witnesses out of court, prior to trial—these are called depositions. Each side can also ask for documents from the other side. At some point settlement discussions may occur which may be handled by a Judge, or by professional mediators. Many factors need to be considered in settling a case such as costs of litigation, the liability of the defendant, how a jury will perceive the credibility of each party, and the effect of a settlement on the reputation of the parties. Most cases actually do settle before trial. Experts may be hired and their depositions taken. Finally, if the case has not resolved, the case will go to trial. There are some cases that are not entitled to a jury trial and the Judge makes the decision. And in some cases, the parties may just agree to have a Judge decide the case. For a jury verdict in a civil case, it takes a minimum of nine out of twelve jurors to win the verdict. The losing party has a right to appeal to the appellate court, a process that usually takes over a year to complete.

How did the woman who spilled coffee on herself at McDonalds win?

It is not appropriate to comment on the merits of a particular verdict, but I can state that cases involving claims that a product was defective in some way may be won or lost on the evidence presented by experts in the particular field, such as the appropriate temperature for serving coffee, and the existence and admissibility of prior claims or complaints by others. On the McDonalds case, most people don't know the whole story. The woman and McDonalds entered into a secret settlement, so we will never know how much she actually got from the litigation.

Why is it difficult to win if you bring a case against law enforcement?

The standard of proof in a case against a law enforcement officer is the same as in other civil cases — a preponderance of the evidence; that is, more evidence than not. A law enforcement officer might win if, for example, the jury finds the testimony of the law enforcement officer more believable than that of the plaintiff. Also, remember that that law enforcement officers have certain legal powers, such as to arrest, and sometimes they are entitled to use force to arrest, a right that the rest of us do not have. So if a person brings a case against a law enforcement officer for using force, that person might not win if the jury thinks the officer was justified in using force.

Do kids get special treatment when breaking the law?

It depends. The law says if you are under 18 years old then you are a minor, a child, (what you and I call a kid), and you are treated differently from an adult.

But if someone is 14 years old or older and he is charged with a very serious crime, like murder or something really violent, then the prosecutor can ask the Judge to have that "minor" treated like an adult. If that happens, the child is prosecuted in adult court and if he is convicted he could be sentenced to state prison, just like an adult.

For most cases (non-serious cases), minors (also known as kids), are not considered criminals. Their cases are handled in civil court, not criminal court. They are handled at the Youth Guidance Center up near Twin Peaks, not at the Civic Center Courthouse or the Hall of Justice.

Kids do not have a right to a jury trial on criminal charges and their case files are not allowed to be shown to the public. But they can still be put in jail. (Incarceration for minors is called "detention," not "jail.")

If the question is whether Judges are not as harsh when they sentence or dispose of the cases charged against kids, that will depend on the crime the young person is found to have committed and whether or not he has a history of committing crimes.

What's the legal age one needs to be in order to file a lawsuit?

18 years old. If people under 18 want to bring a lawsuit they have to ask their parents or other legal guardian to do it for them.

How long does a civil trial usually last?

If the question is how long a civil case takes from the time when you file the complaint to the time when the case is finally done, the answer is that it can take from 1 to 6 years. This is because some cases get appealed after the trial, and sometimes the appeal requires a new trial, which can then result in another appeal. Many civil cases are in fact completed within eighteen months to two years, and an appeal can add another eighteen months or so.

If the question is how long only the *trial* lasts, it depends on how many witnesses testify, how many exhibits are presented, how many defendants are involved and how many questions the attorneys ask the witnesses.

Some trials take a day. Most civil trials are done in two to four weeks. Complicated trials can take two to four months (or more). But remember, in jury trials the jury has to decide the case, and they can take a few days or a few weeks to decide a case after all the witnesses and evidence are presented.

We have rare, very lengthy trials because, for example, the trial might have a long break, such as for one month, to allow the jurors to go on a pre-scheduled vacation. Sometimes the trial is delayed because someone important in the case is sick and takes a long time to get better, so the trial stops and waits for that person come back. Sometimes, there are just a lot of witnesses who need to testify.

What happens to the party that is found guilty? What does it mean 'to be sentenced'?

After a person is found guilty by a jury, the Judge has to make two decisions. The first decision is whether to "remand" someone (which means that he goes to jail immediately and stays there waiting to be sentenced) or to keep him in jail if he has been in custody before and during the trial. The more serious the crime, the more likely it is that the defendant has been in jail up to and through the trial. It is also likely that such a defendant will stay in jail until the sentencing hearing.

One reason to remand defendants is that once convicted, there is a greater risk they will flee and not show up for the sentencing, which usually happens weeks after the trial. Also, depending on the crime and facts of the case, the defendant may represent more of a danger to the community once convicted.

The second thing the Judge must do is set a date and time for sentencing.

When a defendant is "sentenced" the Judge makes a decision about whether the person will be sent to jail or state prison, and for how long. If a person is not sent to jail, he or she is placed on "probation." The Judge determines how long the person will be on probation and what she must do while she is on probation. For example, if someone is convicted of a misdemeanor offense but has prior convictions, or perhaps no serious criminal history, she may be placed on probation, and be required to do community service, pay a fine, attend certain classes for anger management, substance abuse or other conditions.

If someone commits a more serious offense (either misdemeanor or felony), and/or has an extensive criminal history, the law may require that he spend a certain number of years in state prison. The Judge determines what the sentence will be based on a lot of factors set out in the law.

How many times can you be arrested before you go to jail?

It depends. If the arrest is for a serious crime, you usually go to jail and a bail is set. If you post the bail, you are released under order to appear in court for your trial and other court proceedings. If the arrest is for something minor, you get a citation or you are taken to jail, booked but then released, and you are ordered to appear in court at some future date to handle your matter.

Why are some drugs legal while others are not?

The federal government makes the determination about what drugs are considered legal and what drugs are not. The government bases this decision, in part, on whether the drug has any medical purpose, based on research done by scientists. Some drugs are legal only if they are prescribed by a doctor.

Can someone be tried for a crime twice and what is the point of appealing a case?

Usually, a person cannot be tried for the same crime twice. *Double jeopardy* is the legal term for the procedural defense that prevents a defendant (the person accused of the crime) from being tried again for a crime. Take the Giants who won the World Series for example. Once the Giants win the World Series, the games cannot be replayed; the result is final.

The point of appealing a case is to make sure that your case reaches the correct outcome. Judges, lawyers, and jurors are only human, and for that reason, there may be legal errors on rulings in particular cases. The appeal process ensures that the defendant (the person accused of the crime) will not be convicted of a crime based solely on legal error or some other unfair reason.

Now, if a defendant is convicted of a crime, and is successful on his appeal because, for example, the Judge gave the wrong instructions to the jury, the court of appeal might reverse his conviction. In that case, there might be a second trial, this time with the correct instructions.

Being A Judge

Is a Judge allowed to state his/her own opinion or personal perspective about the law?

A Judge maintains many of his/her First Amendment rights to speak generally about his/her opinions. Judges can express opinions about how to improve the legal system. But a Judge cannot state how he/she would rule on a particular case, or on any issue that might come before that Judge. To do so would undermine the confidence of the people that the Judge would have an open mind.

Is choosing someone's sentence difficult?

Yes and it should be. Whether to send someone to jail, prison or release that person into the community is a very difficult decision in many (though not all) cases. Judges have to take into account a number of different factors, such as the sentencing laws, the rights of the victims, the nature and severity of the crime, and facts concerning the convicted person.

Is deciding who is innocent hard?

Deciding who is innocent is nearly impossible. Deciding who is *not guilty* is less difficult, and that is usually the job of a jury. The jury is the fact finder in most cases, and makes the decision as to whether the government proved the guilt of the accused. There are some cases in which the weight of the evidence is overwhelming, and obviously demonstrates guilt. Other cases are more difficult, because there may be evidence going both ways, or perhaps the prosecutor's evidence does not seem very convincing, or perhaps everything depends on whether the jury believes a certain person. Every case is different.

What is the weirdest case you ever had?

In my very first case as a Judge, which was a breach of contract case, the defendant tried to have the case delayed. He came into my courtroom, lay down and claimed that he was unable to get up. After about 30 minutes, we called an ambulance. When the defendant was on the gurney, I informed him that unless he produced a doctor's note indicating that he could not engage in a trial the next day, the trial would proceed. He returned the following day, but the trial proceeded unlike any other trial since. The defendant acted as his own lawyer, and called himself to the witness stand and without notes, he testified for nearly 3 hours. First he would ask himself a question such as, "So Mr. ---, tell about the time that ----". He would then pause dramatically, and then answer his own question.

Why did you become a Judge?

I wanted to become a Judge because I really value the process, respect the rule of law, and wanted to demonstrate my belief that everyone in a courtroom should be treated with dignity, humanity and respect, regardless of what my decision is.

What inspires people to become Judges?

Lawyers with a strong desire to serve the public and help ensure access to justice for all members of our society are often driven to become Judges. And just like the citizens they serve, Judges come from all walks of life. As a result, each has her own unique ideals and life experiences that guide her decision-making. If your goal is to make a difference for your community, a judicial career is one avenue for achieving that goal.

Have any Judges regretted their decisions?

I don't know about other Judges. I have grappled with decisions
before making them and then felt completely unsure if the
decision I made was the right decision. Mostly those
circumstances involve my discretion: decisions that I know will
not be overturned because the ruling was well within the
boundaries set by the law. As for errors in my legal analysis, I
have faith in the higher courts that they will correct me
whenever I mess up.

How do lawyers and Judges ensure their own safety?

Safety is important. As a lawyer, I tried to be ever vigilant about
my surroundings. As a Judge, I am provided with more
security in the courthouse, having the benefit of a deputy sheriff
in my courtroom and secure access to my office. I do not feel as
public as other public figures since, unlike those in the
legislative or executive branch, my name or face rarely appears
in the press. I did endure a stalking case for a few months,
however, and admittedly, until the stalker was arrested, it
caused me a great deal of anxiety.

Has there ever been a case you couldn't solve?

Yes, in a way. For example, in Family Law Court, I must hear
cases because the people who are having the dispute are unable
to reach an agreement. In other words, when people can't agree,
they need a Judge to help them solve their problem. Most of the
time, when they can't agree it is because they want very
different things. Sometimes, both sides are disappointed in my
decision. You might say that these are cases I can't solve,
because no one is happy with the decision I make. But, still,
Judges have to decide every case they are presented with.

What happens when a Judge makes a mistake?

If a litigant feels that the Judge deciding his case has made a mistake, he can first ask the Judge to reconsider the decision, especially if there is new law or new facts the Judge was not previously aware of. If the Judge denies the motion to reconsider, then the litigant my file an appeal with the California Court of Appeal. The Court of Appeal reviews the case and either affirms the trial court Judge or reverses. If the case is reversed it can be sent back to the trial court for further action. If the case is affirmed, the party who lost at the Court of Appeal can file an appeal with the California Supreme Court. In special cases, the California Supreme Court may choose to hear a case after the Court of Appeal has ruled but in most cases those requests are denied.

If evidence is very convincing on both sides, how do you make a decision?

My job is to listen to the facts of the case and apply the law to the facts. Both parties have a chance to present evidence, either testimony from witnesses or documents. Once the parties present the evidence, then I look at the law that I think fits the evidence and apply the law to the case. So even if evidence is very convincing on both sides, generally when I apply the law, one side has a certain type of evidence that helps me make a decision.

There are also rules in the law called *burden of proof.* So the law might say, for example, that the plaintiff (the person bringing the case) has the burden to prove his case. If the evidence is good on both sides, if there is about as much evidence on one side as on the other (or maybe there is really no good evidence on either side!), then the Judge might find that the plaintiff has not sustained his burden of proof, so he would lose the case. When the evidence is as strong on one side as on the other, the party with the burden of proof loses. You can find out who has the burden of proof on an issue by looking it up in statutes, or reading opinions of the appellate courts.

Have you ever had a case that moved to a higher court?

Yes. Everyone who brings a case in front of my court has the opportunity, if they do not like the result, to seek review by a higher court and argue that they are entitled to a different result. Every Judge has seen some of her or his cases appealed to a higher court.

How many cases per week do you preside over?

On average I handle 85 cases per week. Some Judges see more cases than that. Other Judges in a long trial might take, say, three weeks (or more) for a single case.

Do you ever let your opinions affect your rulings?

No. As a Judge, I try not to let my personal opinions or experiences affect my rulings. Judges receive training on ways to ensure that personal opinions do not impact their rulings.

What happens when a Judge has a personal interest in a case?

Normally, a Judge will recuse herself if she has a personal stake in the outcome of a case or some other bias that prevents her from ruling impartially. For instance, if a Judge is scheduled to hear a case in which her close friend is suing a third party, the Judge will opt not to hear the case, and another Judge will preside instead.

If a Judge does not recuse herself and a litigant believes the Judge may be biased, then the litigant may file a motion to remove the Judge from the case. Once the motion is filed, it is assigned to a Judge in a different county who reviews the motion and decides whether or not the Judge from the first county needs to be removed for bias. If the Judge is removed for bias, then another Judge in the first county is assigned to hear the case. Motions to remove a Judge for bias are rarely filed and even more rarely granted.

How many different types of Judges and courts are there?

In San Francisco Superior Court we have about 50 Judges. San Francisco Superior Court Judges are assigned to civil, criminal, juvenile and family law departments. We handle the trials.

Most states have a trial court level, an appellate court, and a supreme court. The appellate and supreme courts are considered "courts of review." The court of appeal reviews the decisions of the trial courts, and parties who lose in the court of appeal can ask the Supreme Court to hear the case. (The Supreme Court may or may not decide to take the case.)

The federal government also has a court system. There too we see trial Judges, who sit in what are called "district court," courts of appeal, and a Supreme Court (in Washington, D.C.).

Are certain Judges assigned to certain cases?

Yes. The Presiding Judge of the Court assigns each Judge to hear a certain type of case. For example, there are family law Judges, civil Judges, and criminal Judges. Judges usually stay in their assignment for several years before being moved to another assignment but the Presiding Judge has the option to reassign a Judge at any time.

What kind of education do you need to have to become an attorney or a Judge?

To become a Superior Court Judge in California, a person must first be a lawyer. Before a person can be a lawyer, he or she must first graduate from law school, which is usually a three year program. Most people go to law school within a few years after they have graduated from college. A Judge must be a lawyer before she or he can become a Judge, but no additional education is required. Most Judges have been lawyers for a long time before they become Judges.

Was it difficult to become a Judge?

Yes. Lawyers must either be appointed by the Governor to be a Judge, or elected by the public. Most Superior Court Judges are appointed by the Governor.

Before applying for appointment to the bench a lawyer must have been a member in good standing of the State Bar for at least ten years and distinguished herself in her area of practice. The lawyer then submits an application to the Governor's office for appointment to the Superior Court. The application is very lengthy and includes questions about the lawyer's trial experience, community service, and commitment to justice. The Governor's office vets all the applicants very thoroughly and seeks input from other Judges, lawyers and community leaders. At the conclusion of the vetting process, the Governor's office interviews a small number of applicants and from those selects the few who will be appointed.

How long do Judges serve?

Superior Court Judges are initially appointed or elected to a 6-year term. The Judges have the option to renew their terms at the end of 6 years unless someone chooses to run for their seat. If someone "challenges" an incumbent Judge then the Judge must run for re-election. Very few Judges have to run for re-election after their initial appointment or election. As a result, most Judges serve for many six-year terms.

Do you feel you have a great deal of power as a Judge? Would you say you use your power responsibly?

Yes, I do feel a great deal of power as a Judge. As a Judge you have the opportunity to make decisions that profoundly affect the lives of the people who appear in court. In order to use that power responsibly, I always try to remember that the people who come to my courtroom are people that need help in solving disagreements, and it is my job to make decisions that best help the people who come to my courtroom, and that comply with the law.

What is the saddest case you ever heard?

The saddest case I ever heard was about a fight that never should have happened in the first place that got out of control and resulted in someone being killed.

What is the longest case a Judge may have to preside on?

It really depends. A case can last for several months, or more. Most cases don't last that long.

What is the hardest case for a Judge to try?

The hardest case for a Judge to try is a case where the attorneys haven't done their homework and aren't prepared. Judges rely on attorneys to know the facts and the law, and to be ready every day to present witnesses and evidence.

What's the hardest part of being a lawyer or Judge?

It is a real privilege and honor to be a Judge, and I enjoy coming to work every day, so this is a difficult question to answer! But there are things that come to mind as I consider what makes it hard to be a Judge. First, as mentioned above, are unprepared lawyers, or lawyers who don't take their work seriously, who are not thinking hard enough about the issues, and perhaps are wasting the time and money of their opponents. The other hard part about being a Judge is that sometimes we have to make decisions which don't really solve the problem, because the problem can't be solved by the law. For example, in family law cases Judges decide which parent will have the kids for what period of time, or how much money one parent has to give the other to take care of the bills, and so on, but these decisions may not be able to fix the real problems of two parents getting along, or at least treating each other with respect. Sometimes, maybe after a victim was seriously hurt or killed, a Judge has to sentence someone to a long term in prison, or make someone pay a lot of money in compensation. But the Judge knows that prison, and money, won't make the pain go away, won't cure anyone, and can't bring back someone who died. These are all hard parts of the job.

Do Judges get extra protection during high profile cases?

Sometimes Judges get extra protection during high profile cases. It depends on the situation, and whether there is a risk to the Judge's safety. Most cases, including high profile cases, do not pose any serious issue about safety for Judges.

Do Judges get to pick what trials they want to hear?

No. Judges have an obligation under the law to handle whatever trial is assigned to them, unless they are disqualified because they have some connection to the case or the attorneys or the parties, or they believe that they cannot be fair and impartial. There are laws that set out the requirements for when Judges must be disqualified.

What is the first case you ever presided over?

The first case I presided over concerned a breach of contract and a real estate broker's commission. I was so unused to being a Judge that, when I politely thanked the lawyer for handing me a trial exhibit, I said, "thank you, your Honor!" I had to explain to the attorneys that I was a brand new Judge, and not yet used to being "your Honor."

How many cases do you see per day?

That varies. If I am in a trial, I only have one trial going on in a day. But I might also have some shorter matters before and after trial, sometimes as many as six. Other kinds of judicial assignments might have dozens (or many more) of very short matters in a day.

What is the average number of cases a Judge may preside on in a month?

The average number of cases depends on what assignment the Judge undertakes. If the Judge has a "calendar court" – one that involves many different people coming to court each day – a Judge may see several hundred people in a month. If the Judge runs a "trial court," then it is possible that a Judge handles one to four cases in a month – depending on the complexity of a trial. Sometimes a Judge will work on one complex case for several months.

What are the most common cases?

There are four main types of cases heard in state court – criminal, civil, family, and probate. Of these categories, criminal and civil cases are the most common. Criminal cases are generally divided into felony, misdemeanors, and infractions. Felonies are the most serious crimes – punishable by state prison sentences. The most common felonies involve drug possession, robberies, and assaults. The most common misdemeanors are driving under the influence of alcohol and petty thefts. Common civil cases are landlord-tenant disputes, personal injury, and employment discrimination cases.

Have two Judges ever tried to sue each other?

Yes. But it rarely involves the work of the court itself. A Judge who is doing his job can rarely be sued for a decision he or she makes. Sometimes, there are private matters between Judges that end up in court. But things relating to a Judge's job performance are usually handled by a disciplinary group composed of Judges and attorneys.

What is a Judge thinking and doing when s/he sits there during a hearing/case?

If the case is tried to a Judge ("bench trial"), the Judge is focused on getting the right answer to the dispute. The Judge might ask questions that allows him to figure out who should win. The Judge is evaluating which witnesses are believable and which are not. If the case is tried to a jury ("jury trial"), the Judge is focused on maintaining order in the courtroom. The Judge concentrates on ruling properly on evidence and running the trial smoothly. The Judge wants to make sure that the jurors are taken care of, that the parties present only fair arguments and admissible evidence. The Judge acts as the guardian of the trial process to make sure that both sides have a fair trial. When the jury convicts in a criminal trial, the Judge starts thinking about the sentencing – the penalties that must be imposed.

When if anytime can a Judge overrule a jury's decision?

Judges are reluctant to overrule a jury's decision. This is because most Judges believe that 12 heads are better than one --

the Judge's! However, there are times when the Judge honestly believes that 12 jurors were misled by improper arguments or allowed their emotions to overcome the evidence that was presented. In those rare instances, the Judge might overrule a jury's decision and allow a new trial to occur. In even rarer occasions, the Judge might completely reverse the jury's decision and enter judgment for the opposite party. In such cases, the originally winning party (and now losing party because of the Judge's decision) will most likely appeal the Judge's decision.

Do Judges get a salary or do they get paid by the number of trials they hear?

Judges get a salary that is fixed by law. Federal Judges cannot get a pay increase unless the United States Congress authorizes it. State Judges also must have legislative approval for any salary increases. Retired Judges can sit as "visiting Judges" to help out overburdened courts. These retired Judges are paid a daily salary.

Why did Judges used to wear wigs? Why do they wear robes now?

According to a famous old book on the law, Blackstone's *Commentaries*, in the early medieval period the only people who could read and write were usually monks, so a Judge making his rounds would stop by the local monastery and have a cleric (clerk) to keep record of the cases tried, parties involved, fines levied, etc. This worked well until the King and the Church got into a dispute, and the King made it illegal for the monks to attend the King's court. In order to prevent postponement of cases, the key court members wore wigs and robes to hide the fact that there was a monk in the courtroom. The wig hid the monk's tonsure (the shaved area on top of his head), and the robe covered his clerical habit. With the Judge and bailiffs dressed in the same way, the monk would not be identified and could participate in court proceedings. In the United States, wigs are no longer worn. The black robe is the sole requirement in almost all states.

Why do Judges wear robes?

The black robe is a symbol of neutrality. It usually does not have any adornment. (One exception was the former Chief Justice of the United States Rehnquist, who wore golden strips on his robes.) The black robe symbolizes the solemnity of the court proceedings. Another ceremonial aspect of the courtroom is manifest when the bailiff (sheriff's deputy) tells people to rise when the court starts each day. Courts are not theaters or entertainment where dramas occur and actors perform (even though sometimes things get quite dramatic and entertaining!). Courts allow people to resolve their disputes. The Judge's black robe sends the message that everyone should take the work of the court seriously because it affects peoples' lives. In criminal cases, someone could end up in jail or prison. In civil cases, someone could lose a lot of money or have her business ruined. In family cases, someone could lose custody of a child. Every time a Judge puts on her robe, she thinks about the important work that she must do and how every case matters to the people involved.

What is the funniest case you ever heard?

I once had to deal with a very large man who participated by telephone because he was too sick to come to court. His opponent was seeking an order to keep him away from his home because the large man never wore clothes around the house. Apparently, he had been an invited relative, who ended up staying too long. I denied the request to issue a restraining order because I concluded that there was no prospect of his doing harm. But I told him that he should put on clothes, especially because there were other family members – including children who passed through the home. He reluctantly agreed to comply.

Lawyers

How much school/training does it take to become a lawyer?

High school diploma or equivalency, together with a college degree. Then you must also graduate from a law school, which usually takes 3 years, and then pass a "bar" exam to be licensed as a lawyer.

How long does a lawyer need to go to school?

Usually a student obtains a four-year college degree and then applies to law school. Most law schools have three-year programs; some have night school programs which take four years to complete.

Is there ever a time when the lawyer doesn't really believe in the side he/she is fighting for?

There are plenty of times that a lawyer does not think that his or her client has a very strong case. If an attorney is working for a law firm, that attorney usually has to represent the client to whom he/she is assigned, regardless of the attorney's personal feelings. Legally, the facts in favor of those companies might actually be very strong, despite the attorney's personal beliefs about a specific product, or behavior, or legal issue. Lawyers do have an important duty to tell their clients if they do not have a strong case. And if a lawyer truly believes that his client has a completely frivolous case, then the lawyer may have an obligation to stop representing that client.

In criminal law and juvenile dependency, things are a bit different. If the Government (in either criminal or dependency) does not think it can meet its burden of proof (that is, does not have a good case), then it is the duty of that Government attorney either to not file a complaint, or to dismiss the complaint once filed. The defendants in criminal cases (or parents in dependency cases) have an absolute right to contest the allegations against them and force the Government to prove its case. For example, even if a lawyer thinks his client is probably guilty of a crime, the lawyer must do everything reasonable to protect his client, and may force the prosecutor to prove, in court, to the satisfaction of a jury, the client's guilt. In these cases, an attorney must fully advise the client on the options and potential consequences related to each decision. Sometimes it might be better not to contest the charges. Ultimately, it is the client's decision as to how to proceed.

If they had the chance would they go over to the other side?

An attorney has an absolute duty to a client he/she represents. This includes maintaining confidentiality and providing effective assistance of counsel and vigorous advocacy. If an attorney cannot provide that for a client, the attorney should withdraw as counsel. Even if an attorney withdraws and no longer represents a client, the attorney is still bound by the attorney/client privilege which means the attorney must keep secret the communications with the client. There are many civil attorneys who represent both defense and plaintiff's sides on cases (but not in the *same* case!). Likewise, there have been many prosecutors who have switched to criminal defense and vice versa over the course of their careers. Lawyers cannot switch sides in the same case because it would be unfair: They would probably have confidential information from the first client which then they might be tempted to use in favor of the other (second) client. This would put the lawyer in an impossible situation, called a *conflict of interest*.

What are some different types of lawyers?

Lawyers work in a wide range of fields and have many different areas of practice. Some lawyers try cases in court; they may be criminal or civil cases. In criminal cases, the People of the State of California are represented by a prosecutor from the Office of the District Attorney. The defendant is either represented by a lawyer in the Office of the Public Defender, or by a private criminal defense lawyer.

In civil cases the lawyers may be in private practice or may work for a non-profit law firm, a corporation (such as an insurance company) or for a government office, such as the Office of the City Attorney or the State Attorney General.

Some lawyers handle family law cases, such as divorces or custody disputes.

Other lawyers provide advice to clients outside court. They may advise on contracts, wills, patents and trademarks, real estate purchases and sales, taxes, employment practices or other business matters.

Some lawyers work "in-house" which means that they are employed by a company to advise about legal matters.

How much $ does the average lawyer make per year?

The national average for lawyers is $45,000 to $145,000, but there is a wide range of salaries. The factors which affect salaries include the number of years in practice, the kind of practice (public interest law firm, government, "in-house" for a corporation, private law firm and whether it is a small, mid-sized or large firm), the lawyer's legal specialty, and the part of the country in which the lawyer practices.

In San Francisco at the largest national law firms the starting salary for a lawyer could be as high as $160,000. A lawyer working in a midsize law firm who has four to nine years of experience on average earns between $106,000 and $163,000 per year. After many years of practice, some lawyers may become partners in a large firm and—those few who are most successful—will earn many millions of dollars per year.

Do lawyers from across sides make deals on the side with each other?

Regardless of the area in which a lawyer practices, the ability to work with other lawyers to resolve issues is important. We refer to this as negotiation.

In court cases, whether civil or criminal, the lawyers often negotiate. They speak to one another to try to settle the case and to avoid going to trial. Approximately 95% of criminal cases are resolved through negotiation and agreement. Frequently, civil cases are settled by discussion between the lawyers for the two sides. In all cases the clients must agree to the terms that the lawyers negotiate, and, if they do, the case is settled.

When two companies or individuals are working on a business deal, the lawyers for each side negotiate with one another to reach agreement, which is usually recorded in a contract.

What is the difference between an attorney and a lawyer?

These terms mean pretty much the same thing. An attorney is a person who handles matters for someone else; an "attorney at law" handles legal matters for her or his clients. Another term for an "attorney at law" is "lawyer."

What kinds of compensation do lawyers get if they win a trial?

Most lawyers are paid on an hourly basis for their services, including trying a case in court. They will get paid the same whether they win or lose. However in some kinds of cases, usually in personal injury cases (such as those arising from an car accident), the person bringing the case (the plaintiff) agrees to pay the attorney a percentage of the amount recovered from the case. This is referred to as a *contingent fee.* If the plaintiff loses the case, his or her lawyer is not paid at all. If the plaintiff wins the case, the lawyer may get 33%, 40% or even 50% of the recovery. This allows plaintiffs who do not have the money to pay an attorney to bring a lawsuit to recover for the injury.

Do lawyers and prosecutors try to hide the truth?

Lawyers have a professional obligation not to present false evidence; they cannot knowingly allow a witness to testify falsely. Lawyers who hide the truth when they are obliged to reveal it, or try to mislead the Court, might lose their license to practice law.

Prosecutors have a legal obligation to provide the defendant and defense counsel with the information that has been obtained through the investigation. It would not be proper for them to hide the truth.

Defendants have a Fifth Amendment right not testify at all. Defendants are presumed to be innocent, and do not have any obligation to present any evidence, even if they know the truth of what happened. However if a defendant or a witness for the defense testifies, she or he must tell the truth.

What are the advantages and disadvantages to choosing not to be represented by a lawyer and representing oneself instead?

The legal system is complicated, and has many very specific rules. Lawyers are trained to follow the rules, and their clients benefit because failure to follow the rules can damage a case, and may result in losing a case which might otherwise succeed. Therefore, it is important to have a lawyer, and it is difficult to identify any advantage in representing oneself. In criminal cases, when a person cannot afford to hire a lawyer, the court provides a lawyer for free because of the importance of having legal representation.

Prisoners

Are the guilty able to say final farewells to loved ones?

In our legal system, defendants have the right to say their final farewells to loved ones. Usually, family members and friends can visit prisoners at certain times and dates.

Do people get charged with any crime if they have a tantrum in court?

If a person has a tantrum in court and is either so disruptive or strikes someone or something, he can be charged with a crime. We hope that never happens. We want the courts to be safe so we have a deputy in all criminal courts to make sure people follow the rules. If they do not obey the rules, the deputy has the authority to either remove them from the courtroom or take them into custody if it gets really bad.

Why does the law care about the well-being of prisoners?

Remember, prisoners are people too. Under the Constitution of the United States, we as a society must insure a minimum standard for how we treat prisoners while they serve their sentence either in jail or prison. Prisoners have a right to humane treatment, medical care, food, and so on. Also, jails and prisons have programs to teach prisoners skills and give them additional education so that when they are released, they can get jobs and hopefully never commit a crime again.

Why would someone be held in solitary confinement?

If someone represents a true danger to himself, other inmates or to prison staff, he can be held in a more isolated area of the prison designated for such individuals. This is done to protect the safety of everyone involved.

How many jails in the U.S.?

I did some research on the internet but I could not find an answer to this question. According to Wikipedia, the "United States has the highest documented incarceration rate in the world. At year-end 2009 it was 743 adults incarcerated per 100,000 population. According to the U.S. Bureau of Justice Statistics (BJS) 2,266,800 adults were incarcerated in U.S. federal and state prisons, and county jails at year-end 2010 — about 0.7% of adults in the U.S. resident population. Additionally, 4,933,667 adults at year-end 2009 were on probation or on parole. In total, 7,225,800 adults were under correctional supervision (probation, parole, jail, or prison) in 2009 — about 3.1% of adults in the U.S. resident population."

There is a distinction between jail and prison. Jails are usually local facilities operated by the city or county. Offenders in jail are usually lower risk and serving a sentence in jail or waiting for trial and have not yet been convicted. Prisons are usually operated by the state or federal government and house the more serious felons. Now that the law has changed in California, only the most serious offenders end up in the prison system. All other lower risk offenders may serve their state prison time in the local county jail.

How many criminals die in jail per year?

I don't know how many prisoners die in jail each year. Again, there are county and city jails and federal and state prisons, each housing a different prison population. Prisoners, like everyone else, get sick and die of illnesses. Some, who are sent to prison for life, will ultimately die in prison.

Are some prisoners allowed to live better lives in jail than others?

It is the goal of people who run the prisons to treat all prisoners with a uniform set of rules. Those rules set out the expectations of the prison staff so that the prisoner knows what conduct may result in disciplinary action and what conduct may be rewarded. If a prisoner follows the rules and demonstrates good conduct, he or she will be allowed to enroll in certain programs or activities as a reward for the good behavior. In addition, the prisoner will keep what is called "good conduct credit" and get out of prison a little earlier than the full time of the sentence.

Do different prisoners get different colored uniforms to wear depending on their crime?

In the San Francisco County Jail, prisoners are dressed in orange jump suits. In federal prison, some wear beige colored clothing. Every jail and prison is different, but all prisoners wear a uniform. Some jails or prisons have the prisoners wear a different color to indicate to the staff something unique about the prisoner. For example, a green shirt in some jails indicates that the person has a hearing impairment.

Sentencing

What is the Judge's final say in convicting someone?

The Judge only has the final say in convicting a defendant (that is, deciding if he is guilty or not guilty) when there is a *court* trial, meaning that the case is presented in front of a Judge alone instead of a jury. When there is a *jury* trial, the Judge acts as a referee; the Judge makes the legal calls, but it is up to the jury to determine the facts. It is up to the jury to determine whether the defendant is guilty or not guilty — which is the same thing as saying it is the jury that convicts, or not.

If a defendant is found guilty (either by a jury or a Judge), the Judge will be the only person deciding the sentence.

Why does the Judge ask if defendants are guilty or not?

The Judge asks the person accused of the crime if he or she is guilty or not because in the United States the defendant is presumed innocent until proven guilty beyond a reasonable doubt. Just because the defendant has been arrested for a crime does not mean the Judge automatically thinks he or she is guilty. The defendant has the right to plead guilty or not guilty when he is told the charges that have been filed against him.

Why are people presumed innocent when we KNOW they are guilty?

The problem is, we *never* know right from the start that someone is guilty. Even if a witness says she saw the defendant do the crime — the witness might be lying. Or perhaps the witness made a mistake, and thought she saw something when, in fact, something else was happening.

A person is presumed innocent because we never know for sure if someone is guilty or not guilty until a trial has taken place, or unless the defendant has decided to admit guilt. There may be facts that suggest the defendant *might* have committed a crime, but that is not the same as finding somebody guilty *beyond a reasonable doubt*, and in the United States no one can be found guilty unless the jury finds him guilty beyond a reasonable doubt.

If, instead of allowing people to have a trial with a jury, we just assumed that certain people were guilty right off the bat, there would be a much greater likelihood that people would be found "guilty" even if they were in fact innocent. Also, even if someone did commit a bad act, there may be defenses the defendant can raise and perhaps get a lesser sentence, or perhaps be convicted of a less serious crime. If we presume the defendant guilty from the start, he or she would not be able to have the opportunity to present these defenses, or his or her side of the story. Have you ever been accused of doing something you didn't do? Perhaps it was another student that violated the teacher's rules, and not you? Didn't you want a chance to explain the situation to the teacher?

Prison

Can the accused sue a Judge or lawyer from jail?

Yes. The accused can sue a lawyer for malpractice or prosecutorial misconduct while in jail. The accused can also sue the Judge, but most defendants have not been very successful. This is because Judges, who are making decisions as Judges, are entitled to do so, whether they turn out to be right or wrong on the law.

What is the difference between bail and bonds and parole and probation?

While bail and bonds both achieve the same purpose of releasing the suspect from custody and ensuring he will return to court, there are some differences.

Bail is a cash payment paid by the defendant to the court. Bail is either paid to the court or promised to the court before the defendant can be released from custody. The amount of bail depends on the type and severity of crime the defendant is accused of committing; typically, the more serious the crime, the higher the bail. The court considers the risk of the defendant fleeing: If the risk is low, the bail is low; if the risk is high, then the bail will also be high. If the defendant fails to return to court as promised, the court keeps the money.

A **bond** is used instead of cash to release someone from custody. The entire bail amount does not have to be paid; only a percentage of the bail amount must be paid. This amount of money, the percentage, which is called the "premium," is usually paid to a "bail bondsman," who guarantees that the entire bail amount will be paid to the court if the defendant does not show up for court. So, for example, if **bail** is set at $10,000, then the defendant may pay, say, a premium of $1,000 to the bail bondsman who in turn puts up the $10,000 **bond**. (The defendant will not get the $1,000 premium back.) If the defendant fails to show up at his court hearing, the bail bondman will try to hunt down the defendant and get him to court, because if he doesn't, the bail bondsman will have to pay the $10,000 to the court.

Probation is a type of sentence, or punishment, after someone is convicted. A defendant is not in jail or prison when he is on probation, but he does have to comply with all the conditions that the Judge imposes. There are strict guidelines that the offender must follow when on probation; if he does not, he risks being sent to jail or prison as a result of the violation.

Unlike probation, **parole** is a conditional release from prison. With parole, the offender has served some time in jail or prison, but is released early based on certain conditions. Again, there are strict guidelines the offender must follow when on parole or else he or she risks going back to prison.

Do famous people or rich people (celebrities or white collar crimes) receive special privileges in court/jail?

No, they do not. Judges work very hard on treating all people equally whether they are a celebrity, rich, poor, a bus driver, a student, or a teacher. While famous or rich people may get more media attention, this does not mean they get special privileges in court or in jail. In fact, in cases with a lot of media attention a Judge will go the extra mile to ensure the person is treated just like every other defendant that comes through the courthouse doors, because the public will be scrutinizing the judicial process.

How often do you think guilty people get away with a crime by some technical mistake made by the other lawyer or the police?

Technicalities are misunderstood, and don't really exist in the criminal justice arena. What people may consider a 'technicality,' such as excluding certain evidence from the courtroom, is really a due process issue. Due process is the requirement that a state must respect all of the legal rights owed to a person. Therefore, if evidence is excluded (and if as a result the case is dismissed), it's because a person's due process rights are being respected. By respecting the person's due process rights even for what some may consider a technicality, we are respecting the Constitution of the United States.

Section II

The *Sunburst* Columns

1. Constitutional Rights

The notion of "constitutional rights" is often tossed about without a good understanding of what it means, and without a sense of the unique position citizens of the United States enjoy as a result of those rights.

This article outlines some of those rights, and suggests a series of issues and questions for discussion. Generally I do not give answers here, keeping the focus on questions, and encouraging readers' thinking on how our underlying constitutional values inform how we think about these questions.

*

Introduction

The idea of "constitutional rights" usually refers to certain rights individual citizens have as against governmental power. These rights are guaranteed by the enduring central document of our nation, the Constitution of The United States — the Constitution of the federal government which reigns supreme throughout the country. States, such as California, also have their own constitutions, and often the rights found there are similar to those in the federal Constitution, but here I'll limit my comments to the federal Constitution.

People referring to 'constitutional rights' usually mean rights in the amendments to the Constitution which became effective in 1791, some years after the original Constitution in 1787 (ratified the next year) but now an integral part it. People usually mean the rights of the First Amendment (to speak, to freedom of religion, to assemble and to petition the government). Or they may mean the Fourth Amendment right to be free of unreasonable searches and seizures; or perhaps the Fifth Amendment right to not be compelled to be a witness against oneself. There are other rights as well, such as to a speedy and public trial, to a jury, and others, but here I'll provide a short discussion of parts of the First, Fourth and Fifth amendments.

But first, a few general points. These rights were originally drafted to be effective as against the federal government- not state governments, not other people, and not companies. After the Civil War, the Supreme Court interpreted the new amendments (the so-called "Civil War Amendments" to the Constitution) to require the First, Fourth, and Fifth Amendments (and others) to also apply to *state* (and local) governments. But it's still true that they only apply as against *government*: no matter what your kids protest, they have no First Amendment right to say anything they want at the dinner table! And one cannot invoke the Fourth Amendment against a *private* company that, for example, searches you on your way into the office (although that might violate other laws).

Another general point. Because these rights are in the *Constitution*, they cannot be taken away or diminished simply on the say-so of Congress, or the President, or other governmental officials. Even a unanimous vote of both the House of Representatives and of the Senate, agreed to by the President of the United States, cannot change the Constitution. The Constitution can be changed only by a formal amendment, which requires the consent of ¾ of the states in the Union.

The First Amendment

The First Amendment actually contains a series of guarantees: free speech, a bar on government establishing religion, a guarantee of free exercise of relation, a right of peaceable assembly, and a right to petition the government. That's a lot, but I'll just focus on the free speech component here.

The title of a book by Anthony Lewis on the First Amendment gets it just right- "Freedom For The Thought We Hate." We don't need guarantees for *popular* speech, or for words or expression that everyone enjoys. We need the First Amendment when the speech is unpopular, or hated, when it makes the community angry – when it's something no one wants to hear. Some of that hated speech is hated for good reason-- perhaps it's racist, or demeaning. For example the Supreme Court has upheld the right of what appears to be a form of religious group to make hateful comments and protest in proximity to military funerals. Sometimes the speech is hateful to a local community, but speaks to a worthy goal: the civil rights protests in Alabama in the 1960s come to mind. The Constitution doesn't pretend to decide whether speech is good or bad, worthy or not – generally we wouldn't want Judges making those sorts of decisions – it just protects the right to speak it all, free of governmental bans.

This doesn't mean that the government can't *regulate* speech- the freedom to speak doesn't block governments from setting reasonable times and places for protests, and doesn't block laws against terroristic threats, blackmail, or breaking into a home to deliver an extortionate demand – all actions which obviously involve some speech.

Drawing the right line between (i) "reasonable" regulation and (ii) regulation that actually interferes with free speech rights can be a very difficult problem, and has led to some very interesting decisions in the courts. For example, past decisions have dealt with issues such as these: Am I within my First Amendment rights to scream "fire" in a crowded theater if there is no fire? Are limits on campaign contributions (e.g., no more than $1000) invalid as restrictions on free speech? Do free speech rights protect the wearing of clothing with rude and offensive words? Does it matter *where* offensive clothing is worn, such as in school, in court, or on the street? If so, who decides what "offensive" means? Are there free speech rights not to wear *any* clothes in public? How about "offensive" books, such as those some might consider to be overtly racist – is there a Constitutional rights to publish them? Distribute them? Distribute them *anywhere*? Are First Amendment rights implicated by governmental requirements that violent video games be labeled in a certain way, or be sold only to people above a certain age?

Fourth Amendment

This provision bans the government from conducting "unreasonable" searches and seizures. (It also has provisions

---

concerning search warrants, which I won't discuss here.) A search or seizure occurs every time a police officers stops a car, or makes an arrest, or TSA stops and searches you at an airport, or the government opens your mail, or places a wiretap on suspected criminals' telephone lines. It happens when the government takes a sample of your blood (they are "seizing" your blood) when you're suspected of driving under the influence. It happens when officers come into your house to search for something, or stop you while riding your bicycle. The sometimes difficult legal question is this: When are those stops and seizures "reasonable" and when are they not?

Usually, the governmental agent (such a police officer) must have some reasonable suspicion that the person to be stopped is connected with some crime. The police cannot randomly stop people, hoping to discover evidence of a crime (such as drugs in their pocket). They need a reason.

The reason might be: a report of a robbery with the description of the assailant—and the officer sees a person who matches the description. Or perhaps a car is weaving all over the road- the officer can stop the car. Perhaps a confidential reliable informant says that a politician is taking bribes- that might be enough to allow the officers to get a warrant to tap the politician's telephone calls.

In some circumstances, the officers don't need any particularized suspicion or reason. Police officers can ask anyone for *permission* to search, and if they get consent—real consent—they can search. Court opinions have also singled out airports as places where searches can take place, even if the officers have no reason to think an individual target has been involved with crime. Part of the theory here is that by deciding to fly, we have in effect 'consented' to the security procedures. By the same token, people are routinely searched coming into courthouses and some governmental offices. Borders are also special places, and the government can search anyone, including for example their bags and computers, as they cross.

In the Fourth Amendment area, there are many interesting issues.

At the time this article was written, the Supreme Court was grappling with a new issue: is it "search" or seizure within the meaning of the Fourth Amendment if police officers place a GPS tracking device on a suspect's car to see where it goes? We know searches without a particular reason can take place at a border — how wide is the "border"? Does that include a location twenty feet past the border gate? Ten miles away on the only road that connects a town to the border? How good a reason must the officer have to stop a man on a bicycle: suppose the man is unwrapping a small piece of silver foil, which looks like it could be drugs — or perhaps an innocent piece of chewing gum? Suppose a man is found walking half a mile away from a shooting at 2 in the morning — can the police stop him on 'reasonable suspicion' of being involved in the shooting? Suppose no one else is around? Suppose there are ten other people around? Is the use of a drug-sniffing dog a "search" that may be protected under the Fourth Amendment?

In all these, and many more, cases, courts must determine what "reasonable" means, in order to decide if there has been a Fourth Amendment violation. Why? How is that courts spend so much time on Fourth Amendment issues? Well, it comes up usually in a criminal case. Evidence has been seized as a result of the stop (or search); say, drugs or a gun has been found on the defendant. The government wants to use this evidence at trial. If the evidence has been obtained as a result of an *illegal* search or seizure i.e., in violation of the Fourth Amendment, the court may "suppress the evidence," that is, ban it from the trial. (This is sometimes known as the exclusionary rule.) Excluding the evidence often results in the dismissal of the charges. Thus it is that courts handle Fourth Amendment issues every day.

Fifth Amendment

Just as with the Fourth Amendment, there are many components to the Fifth Amendment. And again, these are all phrased as guarantees that each of us in this Nation has as against certain kinds of governmental action: action by federal, state, and local officials. I will mention only one of the many Fifth Amendment guarantees here: that which prohibits being compelled to be a "witness" against oneself – the right against self-incrimination. If you are arrested and put on trial for a crime, the government cannot call you to the stand to ask you questions.

Why would this be? Presumably, you as the accused, are in the best position to testify, and know the most concerning whether you are guilty. And we can expect the jury to be very interested in your comments.

The rationale behind the Fifth Amendment guarantee against compelled self-incrimination is fairly obvious: It ensures that suspects will not be coerced, beaten, or otherwise tortured into giving confessions. Not only are confessions given under torture of dubious reliability, but on principle we are revolted by legal systems which depend primarily on confessions, because those systems encourage governmental overreaching, arrests without cause and for ulterior motives, and are not perceived as legitimate by the people. To make sure that governmental authorities do not try to extract confessions in violation of this constitutional amendment, we have, as with the Fourth Amendment, an exclusionary rule. Because we are in particular concerned that confession are voluntary, the courts also require the police to give suspects in custody what are called the *Miranda* warnings (from the name of the case that generated this rule). Why does *Miranda* apply only when suspects are custody? Because being in custody, alone, *is* a form of coercion: people are especially liable to succumb to express and implied threats of pressure under these circumstances. Imagine an exaggerated situation: The suspect is arrested, in handcuffs, in a jail cell, surrounded by twenty police officers with their guns drawn: then one of them asks, "Did you rob the bank?" Would a response really be uncoerced under those circumstances?

Under *Miranda*, therefore, suspects must be *told* they have the right not so speak. If a confession is obtained before the *Miranda* warnings were given (and the suspect is in custody), or if the Judge finds for some other reasons the statement was not voluntary (i.e. there was torture), then the statement is excluded from the trial — the jury will never hear it. This exclusionary rule, like the one that applies under the Fourth Amendment, is designed to ensure there is no incentive for the police to avoid complying with the Constitution.

As with so many constitutional questions, many issues come up in this area. When is a suspect "in custody"? Suppose he is detained for a few seconds while the police check his license—is that "custody"? Or he is handcuffed while waiting for an eyewitness to show up for an identification. Suppose the police think a suspect on the sidewalk is armed and so they approach him with guns drawn—is he really in "custody" yet? Other issues come up with the timing of the *Miranda* warnings: suppose the suspects just blurts out a confession before the police even have time to give the warnings? Should that be suppressed under the exclusionary rule? What is the right result when the warnings are given on one day, the suspect then sits in jail for five days before he is brought into an interview room with seven armed cops and he *then* confesses—should the police have given the warnings again? Does it matter if the suspect, after the original warnings, said he invoke his rights and did *not* want to talk? Does the Fifth Amendment apply at hearings other than criminal trials—for example, can you be compelled to testify at Congressional hearings, or at the trial of someone else? (Hint: No. The rights apply to any governmental compulsions). Is it a violation of your Fifth Amendment rights to be compelled to give a DNA sample, or blood sample?

*

These are only a few of the many interesting, and sometimes difficult, issues of constitutional law that courts across the county must deal with—and we have only outlined a few of the constitutional rights. Sometimes the answers are fairly straightforward; sometimes they are difficult, and reasonable people can differ on the answer. But the bedrock guarantees are there, a permanent and defining feature of our Nation, governed by the rule of law, enforced by our Judges, which no one can ever take away.

---

2.   What Do Lawyers Do?

In the United States, lawyers have usually graduated from college and then gone to a three-year law school before they can become lawyers. They usually also have passed a test called the *bar exam*, which tests their understanding about the law. Finally, people who want to be lawyers must be 'morally fit' to be a lawyer: people with past convictions for crimes may not be able to fulfill this requirement.

If all these requirements are met, the prospective lawyer takes an oath and becomes, as we say, a *member of the bar*. That means the person is a licensed lawyer, and is authorized to practice law. Only licensed lawyers can give legal advice, and act as lawyers in court. (The one exception is when a person does not have a lawyer, and represents himself. This is allowed.) It is a crime to practice law unless one is actually a member of the bar, that is, unless one has actually been licensed. It's interesting to note that Judges are not members of the bar – so Judges cannot give anyone legal advice!

After one has become a lawyer, there is a wide variety of types of work they may do. From just watching television and movies, we might think that all lawyers go to court, and argue cases in front of Judges and juries. This isn't true. Many lawyers work in offices, meeting with clients, researching legal issues, and writing. People hire lawyers because they want to follow the law, and because they want to avoid getting sued in court. They hire lawyers when, for example, they are about to enter a contract and they want to make sure the contract is enforceable in court. They hire lawyers to help them understand the legal requirements in dealing with a governmental agency, or how to comply with the many laws we have, such as those that tell companies how to treat their employees, or environmental laws that regulate the sort of smoke or liquids a company can put into the air or nearby rivers.

Lawyers usually work in one of four kinds of offices.

Some lawyers are hired by a company, and just work for that one client. They advise that one client on various issues, depending on what kind of business the client is involved in.

Other lawyers work for a government, such as a city, or a state, or the federal government. In criminal cases, they might be prosecutors or defense attorneys.

Many lawyers are in what we call 'private practice,' where they have many different clients. In private practice, a lawyer might be the only lawyer in her office, or she might have partners - a few, or hundreds of them, with offices in one location or perhaps in many offices around the world.

Other lawyers work for organizations that are devoted to a certain kind of service, such as clinics that offer free or low rate services to the poor, or to tenants about to be evicted from their apartments, and so on.

Any of these lawyers may have a wide variety of specialties. Some of them might go to court, but many will not. Here's an outline of some of the areas in which lawyers develop expertise (though many lawyers have more than one area of expertise).

- o Antitrust. There are laws that regulate fair competition, for example, laws that prohibit companies from making secret agreements to fix prices. Companies hurt by anticompetitive behavior can sue those who engage in it. Lawyers tell clients how to avoid breaking these laws.
- o Business Law. Companies make agreements all the time, and they need lawyers to draft and negotiate these agreements, and lawyers to sue when the agreements are broken.
- o Criminal. People who are charged with crimes ("defendants") need lawyers to defend them, and the government needs lawyers to handle the prosecutions against the defendants.
- o Dispute Resolution. Some lawyers specialize in out of court dispute resolution. They act as mediators, trying to get

people to agree on a solution, or they are arbitrators, who are essentially private Judges who decide cases, holding their hearings in offices instead of the courthouse.

o Environment and Energy. These lawyers handle contracts and disagreements in the coal, natural gas, and oil industries, and work with (and sometimes against) governmental regulators. Some of these lawyers work on issues involving alternative energy sources such as sun, wind and biodiesel fuels.

o Family Law. In this area lawyers help families which are going through divorces, and they try to negotiate issues (or argue on the issues in court) about dividing the family property and money, and responsibilities for children.

o Immigration. Immigration lawyers help people who are not citizens of the United States in applying for entry into the country, the papers needed to stay in the country legally, and helping them become citizens.

o Intellectual Property Law. Intellectual property includes patents, trademarks, trade secrets, and copyrights.

   o Patent lawyers draft up descriptions of inventions (perhaps a new kind of water pump, or engine, or software, or other useful product), and get the U.S. Patent Office in Washington, DC to approve the patent as something which really is new. If so, then the patent holder owns the invention, and can get money from others who want to make the invention (or the patent holder can make the invention herself, and stop others from doing so).

   o Trademarks are symbols, like the big yellow "M" arches for McDonalds, or the "Just Do It" tag line for Nike shoes, or the scripted words "Coca-Cola" for that soda drink. The owners of trademarks can resister their marks with the government, and stop other people from using the marks in a confusing way—for example, from using the marks on fake products.

   o Trade secrets are secrets about how to do something, or secret ingredients, that give a company an advantage over other companies. An owner of a trade secret may be able to stop others from making it public.

o Copyrights apply to things people write such as songs, poems, novels, video games, plays, movies, and other art. Others usually cannot copy these creations without permission.

Intellectual property lawyers help people protect their rights by filing the right kind of papers with the government, and suing others who violate the rights. Sometime these lawyers also specialize in an industry, such as music, or video games, or other computer software or hardware.

o Labor and Employment Law. These lawyers handle relationships, agreements and disputes between employers and employees, and groups of employees known as "unions" which negotiate with companies for pay and other aspects of their employment such as workplace health and safety and retirement programs.

o Real Estate. These lawyer spend their time on the purchase and sale of land and buildings. They work for a variety of people and companies involved in real estate, such as sellers and buyers, and the banks that loan money to allow people to buy property.

o Trust and Estate Law. These lawyers help people make wills, and they also draft up documents which create "trusts" which are legal entities than can own property. These lawyers also litigate in court problems that arise under the wording of wills and trusts.

o Taxation. Tax lawyers help people with their taxes, and come up with legal ways to minimize taxes. Sometimes they handle lawsuits in which the government wants more taxes paid and the taxpayer denies that he owes any more taxes.

o Tort. Sometimes people are injured on the job, or in car accidents, or during a medical procedure, or as the result of exposure to drugs, chemicals, asbestos, or other dangerous items. If so, they may hire a tort lawyer to take their case, to sue the people responsible for the injury. These lawyers spend a lot of time in court.

This is just a small sampling of the types of work lawyers do. Lawyers are advocates, and they are expected to vigorously protect their clients, and to do whatever they legally can to help their clients. At the same time, all lawyers are "officers of the Court," which means that, no matter what, they have to be honest and forthcoming with the Judge. Lawyers may never try to mislead the Judge, and may never try to hide evidence when there is an obligation to reveal it. Lawyers' first and highest responsibility is to the preservation and integrity of the legal system.

3.   How Judges Become Judges

Both the federal and state governments have Judges. Federal and state Judges go through different procedures to get the job, although typically all Judges have previously been lawyers. There is no minimum requirement for federal Judges, but California state Judges must have been lawyers for at least ten years. More typically, Judges have been lawyers for about twenty years, although there are many exceptions, with some Judges appointed about ten years after they take the bar exam after law school, which means they might be no more than 35 years old. Our past Chief Justice, Ronald George, was 32 years old when he was first appointed Judge at the trial court level (he was later appointed to the intermediate Court of Appeal, and then later to the state Supreme Court).

California State Court Judges

State trial Judges are Judges of the Superior Court. There is a Superior Court in each county of the state. Lawyers can become Superior Court Judges in one of two ways: They may run for office and be elected in their county; or they may be appointed by the Governor. Superior Court Judges have six year terms, which means that every six years, they have to stand for re-election (even if they were first appointed). Any lawyer can run against a Superior Court Judge when the Judge seeks a new six year term. Sometimes, Judges will retire just before their term expires, and then any lawyer can run for that vacancy. It can be difficult and expensive to run for office, so as it happens there are relatively few Judges who get the job through the election process.

More commonly, the Governor appoints trial Judges. A vacancy might arise through retirement, death, or when a Judge is elevated to the Court of Appeal. The Governor has an online form which applicants must fill out. There are many questions, and the form asks for tremendous detail about one's qualifications for the job.

—

You can see the form for yourself at
http://gov.ca.gov/s_judicialappointments.php. It can take weeks
to develop the materials requested. The form is sent to the
Governor, who has it reviewed with the help of his staff. If it
appears that the applicant may qualify, the Governor sends the
name of the applicant to the Commission On Judicial Nominees
Evaluation. (Often Governors send out more than one name per
vacancy to the Commission.) The Commission includes lawyers
and non-lawyers, and it is required to investigate the candidate.
The Commission does this by meeting with the candidate, doing
background research and sending out questionnaires to hundreds
of people, including other lawyers, who know the applicant.
Eventually the Commission reports back to the Governor that the
applicant is qualified, or highly qualified, or (in some cases) not
qualified. The Governor is not bound by this rating, but uses it as
he or she decides. If the Governor is still is interested in the
applicant, an interview is arranged at the capital in Sacramento.
Eventually, the applicant may get a phone call from the Governor's
Office call that he or she has been appointed. The call can come
very soon after the interview, or it might come a long time later--or
it might never come at all. Unsuccessful candidates simply do not
hear back.

Governors always appoint the members of the Court of Appeal and
the Supreme Court; one cannot be elected to those offices. The term
of office is 12 years, and so every 12 years the voters decide whether
to keep the Court of Appeal or Supreme Court justice; or not. This is
termed a *retention* election. If the justice is not retained, there's a
vacancy and the Governor can appoint someone else. The
appointment process is similar to that for trial Judges, but with an
extra step. Once the Governor has decided on the applicant, the
name is then sent to yet another Commission- the Commission on
Judicial Appointments. This Commission is always made up of
three people: The Chief Justice, the Attorney General, and the
presiding justice of the Court to which the applicant has applied.
The Commission has a public hearing, at which people for and
against the candidate can testify. If this Commission votes in favor,
then the candidate is sworn into office as an appellate justice (or
justice of the Supreme Court). Generally, justices on the Court of

Appeal come from the Superior Court, and the Supreme Court gets its members from the appellate court. But there's no rule on this, and the latest member of the Supreme Court is Goodwin Liu, who previously never had been a Judge.

Federal Court Judges

Federal Judges are sometimes called "Article III" Judges, because the Constitution of the United States, at Article III, provides for the judicial branch, and also gives federal Judges life tenure. That means that federal Judges never have to run for office, and (with the exception of impeachment, which I'll discuss in a moment) can never lose their jobs. In this way the Founders of our nation sought to ensure the complete independence of federal Judges. The Founders understood that Judges sometimes have to make unpopular decisions — and that they need to be able to do that without fear of losing their jobs.

The President of the United States appoints all federal Judges. But in practice, people interested in becoming federal trial Judges, known as District Court Judges, apply to their Senator. The 100 United States senators all have different ways of evaluating these candidates, but many use groups of lawyers they trust to sift through the applications, and to make recommendations. The Senator then sends the names of his or her choices to the President of the United States. Especially if the Senator is of the same political party as the President, the President normally follows the Senator's recommendation. Usually the applicant is invited to the White House for an interview with a lawyer who works for the President, and the FBI conducts a background investigation, speaking with the applicant's family, friends, and business acquaintances. If the President approves, the applicant is nominated and his name is provided to the Senate of the United States. There, the Senate Judiciary Committee holds hearings, perhaps listening to the candidate and witnesses for and against the appointment. The name is then "reported out" of committee to the full Senate, which then votes on the appointment: a majority vote is enough to confirm the candidate. The Senate, however, may or may not take a vote, depending on innumerable political reasons (some of which may have nothing to do with the candidate's qualifications). But no one can become a federal Judge without being nominated by the President and confirmed by the Senate.

Candidates for the federal Courts of Appeals are treated similarly, although Presidents have a more central role in their selection, and ideas for nomination can come from not only Senators but a wide range of other sources. And Presidents take the central role in picking United States Supreme Court justices, consulting with anyone they want. The President will usually himself interview the applicant. But again, the candidate is nominated by the President and must be confirmed by the Senate.

As I mentioned, federal Judges cannot be removed from office except by impeachment. Some people use the word 'impeachment' to refer to the entire process of removing the Judge from office, but technically 'impeachment' just mean the filing of charges, the first step in actually removing the Judge. The House of Representatives conducts an investigation, often has hearings, and then impeaches the Judge by filing formal charges. This might be done, for example, if the Judge took bribes, or other crimes. After the House impeaches, the case is transferred to the Senate of the United States, where there is a trial with the Senators sitting, in effect, as the jury. If the Senate votes to convict, then the Judge is removed from office. Impeachment is very rare. Only about fourteen Judges have ever been impeached and removed from office.

Selection Criteria

Sometimes when people ask how lawyers get to be Judges, they are not asking about the process. They are asking what it takes to be appointed, what sort of background one should have, whether politics matter, whether it helps to "know someone."

There's no general answer. Every Judge has a different story. Different Presidents and Governors look for different things. It's true that some people get appointed because of a close relationship with a President or Governor, and it's also true that some are appointed after long service to a political party or politician. Some

Governors tend to appoint certain kinds of lawyers; for example, under some California Governors, former prosecutors may have had an easier time getting appointed than criminal defense attorneys. And typically, trial experience counts for quite a lot (many lawyers have never seen the inside of courtroom), although that seems to be changing, with more attention to a wider set of legal skills.

But my guess is that most California state Judges who were appointed had little contact with the political process. On my court, we have former defense attorneys, prosecutors, city attorneys, attorneys from small firms and from very large firms, lawyers who specialized in plaintiffs' case and those who specialized in defense cases. Some spent a lot of time volunteering for the courts as temporary Judges; some spent enormous amounts of time on state and city bar activities (the "bar" is shorthand for lawyers as a group, who are admitted to the "bar"), involved in education, training, and civic functions. Some joined committees that reviewed and proposed new laws and rules for the courts. Some spent most of their time as lawyers in federal court, others never had a federal case. For most Judges, there's no great secret to their appointment: they stood out as lawyers. Over time, others began to see them as reliable, honest, hard working, and with a lot of common sense—in a word, they built up a good *reputation*. The Judges I know have something else in common, too: they care a lot about public service. They have been involved in community activities, or trying to improve the justice system, for years before they became a Judge. And they probably became a Judge precisely because public service was so important to them.

4.   Jury Service

The American form of government, and especially its court system, is the envy of the world. In other countries, such as those in the Middle East, people fight and demonstrate, and are willing to die, for what we take for granted.

Ignorance about the law exacts a high price. Citizens do not know their rights. People are frightened by the system, and intimidated by those who seem to know their way around the courts. Folks looking for lawyers are not good consumers: They don't know what questions to ask of their potential advocate. Business people make bad decisions, not knowing when to seek legal counsel. Ignorance makes gibberish out of public debates about significant issues such as abortion, gay marriage, crime and sentencing, or why juries produce certain verdicts.

Ignorance about the courts reduces public support for the courts, too, which can diminish legislative funding for the courts, which in turn reduces court services. Reduced court services are bad all around: longer lines at clerks' windows, delays to get to trial, greatly increased expenses, and more frustration.

And, too, ignorance about our courts leads to high anxiety about jury service, sometimes anger as a result of being called to serve, and frustration at what seems to be a long and tedious process.

*

I have noticed a stunning difference in the views of those who end up actually serving on a jury versus the group (we call them the "panel") as they first appear in the court room. When the fifty or sixty folks first appear in my courtroom, many on the panel are anxious, sometimes upset to be called away from their daily personal and business routines. But by the end of the trial, jurors are almost always happy to have served, and they have good things to say in their post-trial questionnaires. They are pleased to have performed a public service--for perhaps the only time in their lives.

How is this? The jurors who have served understand something that the panel does not. The jurors found out that jury service is rewarding, intense, and sometimes even exhilarating as one discovers the truth of how the justice system works, and how twelve citizens from all walks of life and backgrounds come together to reach a just result. Because of their experience, these jurors have lost their fear and apprehension. They know they can rely on common sense, they have the law the Judge provided to decide the case, and they have the impressions and thoughts of fellow jurors as they decide whom to believe and which witnesses to rely on. They know the job.

Why Juries?

Those who end up on a jury understand how our justice systems works, what happens at a trial, how the truth comes out. They see the Constitution in operation — in a way, they become the living embodiment of our Constitution.

The right to a fair and impartial jury is one of the most important guarantees of the Constitution. It is at the core of the justice system. It is what distinguishes our country, as a nation under law, from most of the governments in the world and throughout history. But constitutional rights only exist as long as there are people who are willing to uphold them and fully participate in the process.

There are no juries in India, Israel, or Sweden. In Iran, trial is before an appointed Judge who answers to the powers that run the government. There are no juries in Switzerland. There are few juries even in England (where our jury right came from) except for the most serious crimes, and certain types of civil cases. In Viet Nam, the Judges are approved by the communist party.   In China the government decides whether a defendant will have access to a lawyer and usually the witnesses are not available to be cross examined in court.

The court systems may work well in many of these countries such

---

as Israel, England, Sweden, and India. But the U.S. system is unique in the safeguards it affords through the use of juries.

In the United States we have *independent* courts which resolve disputes between people and between companies, and which guarantee people's constitutional rights and render verdicts based only on the facts and on the law. Our courts are independent because they are not answerable to presidents, or other politicians, government officials, generals, dictators, or the local militia. Our courts answer only to the law, the law as enacted by the people — that is, the same people who show up for jury duty.

Jury Selection

Generally courts obtain the names of prospective jurors through DMV records and voter registration lists. A random selection is asked to come in, and generally meet first in the court's jury assembly room. Hundreds of people may be assembled there. Groups of about 50 or 60 people are then selected at random to go to a Judge's courtroom. The Judge welcomes the panel, says a little about the case and how long it is expected to be, and then asks general questions designed to see if any member of the panel is biased or prejudiced for or against one of the parties. "Prejudice" here doesn't have just the ordinary meaning, but also refers to a sense that a prospective juror doesn't have an open mind about some important issue, or has a strong feeling which he or she cannot put aside. The point is simply that the jury can be made up only of folks who will decide the case solely on what happens inside the courtroom, solely on the presentations of witnesses and documents; and not based on a past experience of a juror. After the Judge is done, the lawyers have a right to ask questions too, perhaps following up on the Judge's questions, or asking others. Again, the only point here is to make sure jurors don't have such strong feelings about an issue that they can't be open to the evidence-and only the evidence — presented in the courtroom, and to ensure they will actually follow the law as provided to them by the Judge.

When asked questions, jurors can discuss private responses with the Judge and the lawyers outside the hearing of the other people in the courtroom.

After the questions, the Judge and lawyers take a break and discuss the responses of the panel, and make suggestions as to people who might, for example, automatically vote one way or the other, regardless of the evidence. Some people simply shouldn't sit on certain juries, because it wouldn't be fair to one of the two sides.

Back out in the courtroom, the Judge may excuse some of the panel, and then the Judge allows the lawyers to exercise what are known as "peremptory challenges" to the panel. This just means each lawyer is allowed to exclude a certain number of people. Although no reason need be given, lawyers can't do this based on race, sex, gender, race, ethnic origin and so on. The goal is simply to give each side a chance to have some role in the choice of the people who will ultimately decide their case; in this way, regardless of how the jury votes, even the losing side is more likely to accept the result, good or bad. When the peremptory challenges are done, the first 12 of the remaining people are the jury, and generally a few more are picked as alternates.

The entire process can take a day, and sometimes more. It can be tedious to sit and listen to the questions addressed to someone else in the room. But there's no short cut. Every person who might end up on the jury needs an opportunity to discuss his feelings, thoughts, and backgrounds with the Judge and the lawyers. Sometimes, it turns out that a person who seemed to be entirely neutral has deep-seating feelings about a key issue that he or she simply cannot set aside; sometimes, we find that a person who seemed to automatically favor one side in fact *can* be fair, and *is* open to the arguments of both sides. It just take time to figure this out.

The Job

So what do jurors do? They are Judges, Judges of the facts. Juries decide what happened. They decide based on the evidence they see and hear in the courtroom, and the legal instructions the Judge provides. They listen to witnesses, and decide how much weight to give to that testimony. They might listen to what we call percipient witnesses — witnesses who saw or heard something related to the case. They might hear expert testimony, perhaps on handwriting identification, how alcohol affects the body, the way in which a hip implant works or is removed, or some other kind of scientific testing.

Jurors can take notes, and in many courtrooms, including mine, they can ask questions of the witnesses (by submitting short written questions to the Judge). Juries are strictly forbidden from making their own investigations or experiments or research, including on-line research, on any aspect of the case. Jurors cannot research the facts, or the law, or the people, involved in the case. Why? Because then the verdict might not be based solely on what happens in the courtroom, and one party or the other would then have been cheated of a fair trial. In a fair trial, the parties know what the evidence against them is, and have an opportunity to rebut or contradict it.

Juries are neutral, they are fair, they are open minded. Their verdicts are based solely on the evidence presented in the courtroom, and the law the Judge gives them. It is a serious work, but it is not a hard job — millions of Americans do this every year. And — as it turns out — they enjoy the public service, and the sense that one has, even for a brief period, exercised the sovereign authority of the government, and personally implemented the Constitution.

5.   Who *Are* Those People In The Courtroom?

It is a confusing experience to walk into a courtroom. Various people are seated at various tables, papers are shuffled, handed up to the Judge, and shared among others. Everyone seems to be doing something different, yet somehow they all seem to handling aspects of the same case. In some busy criminal courts, some people are talking among themselves to the side of the courtroom while the Judge is talking to a different set of people. Everyone seems to be madly scribbling on paper or concentrating on their computers. While some courts are peaceful and serene, other courts are a hive of activity with scores of people — some in suits or skirts, others in orange jumpsuits — taking turns at a small lectern talking to the Judge with incomprehensible phrases (sometimes just a string of numbers), a sort of code that everyone else seems to understand. From the public seats in the back of the courtroom, these discussions with the Judge may be hard to understand not simply because of the strange words, but also because the sound system in the room simply makes it difficult to hear the voices.

The first step in understanding what is happening in a courtroom is to understand the job descriptions of the people involved.

The Jury. If you are visiting a jury trial, you will see along one side of the room a group of twelve people, sometimes more, on chairs behind a railing or bar. This is the jury. They sit in what is often called the *jury box*. We usually have 12 person juries, and often we have two or more alternates (in case one of the twelve gets sick), bringing the total to 14 or more. The jury decides who wins and loses the case.

The Judge. The Judge is probably sitting at the far end of the room, likely on raised platform behind what we call the "bench."   The bench is in fact a large desk on which the Judge can place her books and notes. The Judge usually runs the courtroom proceedings, deciding when the next issue or the next case is going to be called, and making decisions on who wins or loses in the hearing. In a jury trial, the Judge tells the jury what the law is. The jury decides what the facts are (did the defendant take the money? Did Bob really promise to sell a house to Debby and then fail to do so? And so on.). Using the law from the Judge, the jury decides who wins and loses; so for example the jury would decide if the defendant was guilty of theft, or if Bob breached a contract. In criminal cases, only the Judge decides on what the sentence is going to be (a sentence such as so many days in jail, the fines, and/or probation).

The Clerk. The clerk has a lot of different jobs. Sometimes the clerk calls the cases, which means telling people who are in court that it's their turn to come up to face the Judge and be heard. The clerk takes detailed notes on who participated in a case, what happened, and the time when it happened. So, for example, the clerk will record when a witnesses started testifying, or when a piece of evidence (such as a document) was admitted into evidence (which means it became a part of the case and could be relied on by the Judge or jury to decide issues). The clerk will record the Judge's actions, such as dismissing a case, or granting or denying some other request. The clerk usually administers the oath, making sure each witness swears to tell the truth. During jury trials, the clerk does a lot of support work for the jury, answers their questions, ensuring they have documentation for their employers, and so on, as well as taking care of evidence submitted to the court. Clerks file documents, which means the clerk stamps them, making them a part of the official record, and makes sure the documents get into the proper files. He also files the Judge's orders, and sends these out to the people who are affected by the order. You will probably see the clerk seated close to the Judge, because he will often be exchanging papers with the Judge.

The Bailiff (also known as the deputy, or deputy Sherriff). Bailiffs are in uniform, and they make sure everyone is safe in the courtroom. Especially in criminal trials, bailiffs are important to ensure there is security. In some kinds of other cases, too, such as Family Court (where emotions can run high), bailiffs are often present to make sure all participants keep their tempers in check.

More generally, bailiffs ensure the security of the courthouse, and usually operate metal detectors at the entrance of the courthouse. Bailiffs also take charge of juries when they are deliberating, to stop any attempt to influence the jury while it is discussing and deciding the case.

The Witness. In trials, someone is probably testifying, giving evidence in the form of sworn oral testimony. A witness is someone who knows something relevant to a case: perhaps an eye-witnesses, or someone otherwise involved in the events leading up to the lawsuit. Expert witnesses also testify. These are people who have an expertise such as finger-print examiners, laboratory technicians, accident reconstruction experts, doctors, and so on. Usually the witness is seated close to the Judge, facing either the jury or facing out into the courtroom.

The Court Reporter. The court reporter is probably seated close to the witness chair, which in turn is probably next to the Judge, perhaps on the other side of the room from the Clerk. The reporter takes down everything everyone says in a hearing or trial, in a sort of shorthand which is usually saved in a computer file. Sometimes the Judge can see what the court reporter is typing—the Judge may have a computer screen on the bench connected to the reporter's machine, and in this way the Judge can read what someone said. The reporter's notes are also used at the end of the trial, while the jury is deliberating, such as when the jury asks for a "read back" of a witness's testimony. This can be very useful when the witnesses testified, for example, a week or more in the past. The main function of the reporter's notes, however, is to create a *record on appeal*. When a losing side wants to appeal, the reporters' notes are transcribed onto paper, and in this way the court of appeal can see exactly what everyone said, what the Judge's rulings were, and so on. This allows the court of appeal to see if there were any serious mistakes made at the trial, and helps the appellate court decide whether or not to reverse the result in the trial court.

Counsel for the Plaintiff (or for the People). In a civil cases, where one person or company is suing another, the party bringing the case is called the plaintiff. In a criminal case, it is always the People (the government) which commenced the case. The party bringing (or starting) the case, whether a plaintiff or the People, always sits at the table closest to the jury box, facing the Judge. At that table you will find the lawyer (also known as 'counsel' or 'attorney') for the People or plaintiff. That lawyer might be seated next to his or her client. Sometimes there are many lawyers at counsel table.

Counsel for the Defendant. The party defending the case in a civil suit (the person or company that was sued), and the party defending in a criminal cases (the person who got arrested) is the defendant. He, and his lawyer, will be found at the tables farthest away from the jury. If you are visiting a criminal court which is not in trial (e.g. with a jury), you may be watching the Judge handle a large number of cases back to back, handling various *pre*trial aspects of the case. In such cases, defendants may be in custody, and are identifiable by their jail clothing (such as an orange or blue jumpsuit), or they may be handcuffed. Some defendants will not be in custody, and will appear in ordinary street clothes. They will appear with their lawyers on one side of the courtroom, with the prosecutor on the other side, as they briefly argue issues such as bail, whether the prosecution has turned over the evidence to the defense, when the case will be sent out for trial, and so on. Sometimes the defendant will make a plea bargain, pleading guilty to some charges in return for a certain sentence. A Judge might handle, say, 30 or 50 such cases in a morning.

Other seating in the courtroom. Some courtrooms have a few rows in the front of the public seating reserved for lawyers who are waiting their turn to speak to the Judge. In many courtrooms, there is a railing (or bar) which runs across the courtroom, separating public seating from seats reserved for lawyers, their clients, and others directly involved in the case.

Other staff. Much of the work of the courts is actually done by people whom you will not see in the courtroom. But without them, we would not have a justice system. We have clerks who take papers to be filed, file them, and take information from those papers to put into our computer systems. We have folks who operate the computers and websites and maintain software we need to do our work. We have additional deputy sheriffs who transport prisoners to and from courtrooms and jails. We have lawyers and law students who help Judges with legal research. We have staff who handle personnel issues- the same issues regarding employment, insurance, and so on, that any business has to take care of. We have people handling our budget. We employ coordinating supervisors who assign other staff to various parts of the court and different courtrooms. We have staff helping with the training of our clerks and Judges, clerks who keep track of the status of our many thousands of cases and send out official notices and orders, as well as clerks who prepare cases for appeal, making copies of papers, collecting fines and fees, maintaining evidence and exhibits, and helping the public and the media review our public records. You will rarely meet these people, but they are the core that keeps the rest of us able to run the courts.

6.   What is a Trial?

People get into arguments, and sometimes they disagree. If they cannot resolve their disagreements, they may ask someone else to step in and resolve the dispute. They may ask a trusted friend, or kids might ask a parent or favorite aunt to solve the problem. In school, a teacher or administrator may help resolve disagreements. In an office, a supervisor, or perhaps the president of a company, might decide who is right and who is wrong.

Disagreements about who should be elected to Congress or the state legislature, or who becomes President of the United States, are all resolved by voting. Disagreements about which is the best baseball team are resolved by playing in the World Series (admittedly, there are other ways to determine great baseball teams!). Some disagreements can be worked out only through negotiations, a sometime slow process of meeting, discussing, arguing, and compromising to get things done. For example, a lot of work in the legislatures is done this way, as well as many of the disputes which are brought to the United Nations.

There are other ways to resolve disputes, too. War, or other violence, sometimes resolves disputes over land, natural resources, religion, political power, and so on. Where there are no governing rules, or no higher authority to appeal to, sometimes people do anything they want to get their way, including attacking others who disagree with them. When physical force is used, the person with the best weapon wins, no matter who is really right, or who has the better argument.

We form governments, and impose rules on ourselves, to (among other things) avoid violence. We form treaties with other nations, and join organizations such as the United Nations, to avoid war. For certain types of disputes, when the parties cannot work out a solution on their own, we provide the court system to provide a final resolution. A trial is the way these disputes get resolved.

Courts provide solutions peacefully, with dignity and respect, and in a way that makes sure everyone is heard, and everyone is treated fairly.

Cases In Court

Not every dispute can be brought into the court system. And even disputes which are ordinarily eligible to be in court might actually get resolved *outside* of court. I'll discuss those situations later in this note.

Only certain cases can be the subject of a trial in court. The legislature defines the sorts of cases that can be filed in court. There are two basic types: civil and criminal. Criminal cases are filed when someone violates a criminal law- for example, a law that says you can't drive while you're drunk, or can't steal, or can't hit someone else. Civil cases are usually disputes about money or other property, for example, a dispute whether someone owes another some money (e.g., the boss owes you a salary and never paid it), or failed to abide by an agreement to sell a house or other item. You can also sue if someone hurts you in, for example, a car accident: you sue to recover what you paid for medical treatment, to fix the car, and to compensate you for your pain.

People with these disputes do not, however, *have* to go to court. They might agree to submit the case to a neutral person to get it decided. These neutrals are called arbitrators. If everyone agrees, arbitrators can take over and decide the case. Judges respect the right of people to come up with their own peaceful ways to resolve disagreements. But if they can't agree on a method, the case goes to court.

What happens at trial

I'll describe a typical civil jury trial. As I noted above, *civil* cases are lawsuits involving people or companies (or sometimes the government), usually when one side wants money or other property from the other side. Let's assume Bob sells Ann a car. Ann pays money, let's say $20,000, for the car. A week after the sale, the car breaks down: It turns out the engine is bad: perhaps it's rusted, or too old. Ann doesn't want the car now: she wants her $20,000 back; but Bob won't give it back. He says she should have inspected the car, and he never said it actually would work anyway. Ann says Bob told her the car was in great shape. They can't agree on how to resolve the dispute, and Ann sues Bob in Superior Court. She claims fraud, breach of contract, and so on.

Ann and Bob show up on a fine Monday to try the case. They (and their lawyers) are assigned to a specific Judge in the courthouse for trial. They discuss a few pretrial issues with the Judge; perhaps they have an argument about whether a particular pieces of paper—say, Bob's notes about his sale to Ann—will be seen by the jury. This poses a legal issue the Judge will decide.

Then a group of about 50 people are called up from the jury assembly room—where earlier perhaps 200 people showed up for the various trials to start that day—to the Judge's courtroom. These 50 people are the "panel." The Judge tells the panel a little about the case, and then asks a series of questions designed to find out if they can be fair to both sides. Perhaps one of the panel is in fact right in the middle of her *own* dispute with a car dealer—she might not be fair to Bob. Perhaps one of the panel is a car dealer, or is married to or lives with a car dealer: he might not be fair to Ann. Someone might not understand any English, and someone else might have to be at a funeral on a day the trial is supposed to be in session. The Judge may have to let these people go.

The lawyers get to ask questions too. This process of asking questions to see how people feel, and to get a sense of whether they can be fair to both sides, is called "voir dire." The Judge lets go the people he thinks might not be equally fair to both sides. The lawyers then also get a chance to let some of the people go: they exercise "preemptory challenges" which means they can, for almost any reason, let people go who they think might be a problem. (They *cannot* excuse people based on race, religion, sexual orientation, and so on.)

After the Judge and the lawyers have excused those people, the first 12 people left over, picked in random order, are the jury. The Judge might also take a couple of people as alternates, to fill in if one of the 12 gets sick during the trial.

Then the lawyers make opening statements, telling the jury what the case is about, why they are there, and what they think the evidence will prove. The plaintiff — the person who brought the suit (here, Ann), puts on her evidence first. (Actually it will be Ann's *lawyer*, if she has one. From here on, I will just say Ann or Bob, although I usually mean their *lawyers*.) Evidence is usually the testimony of witnesses under oath; or documents. When Ann asks questions of her witnesses it's called *"direct* testimony." The other side (Bob) gets to *cross examine* Ann's witnesses. Ann might then ask some follow up questions of her witnesses (that's *redirect*).

When Ann has finished obtaining testimony from all her witnesses, she "rests," and Bob gets his chance to put on his case. He calls witnesses on direct, asking them questions. Ann gets to cross examine. Bob gets to ask follow up questions of his witnesses. When Bob is finished, he rests, and Ann gets one last chance (in a part of the trial that is called "rebuttal") to put on evidence that contradicts what Bob's witnesses said.

When Ann is done, the Judge instructs the jury on what the law is. He will consult with Ann and Bob in trying to find out what the law is, and Ann and Bob might have a disagreement on the law. It's the Judge's job to figure out the law. He does this by reading approved jury instructions, from cases written by other Judges, and from reading the statutes passed by the legislature.

Then the Judge instructs the jury. For example, the Judge might tell the jury that to prove fraud, Ann must prove that (1) Bob said something about the car (2) which was false, (3) Bob knew it was false (4) Bob intended that Ann rely on what he said, and (5) what Bob said would be important to anyone buying a car. (I don't mean this is actually the law — I just made this up as an example.)

When the Judge is done with instructions, the lawyers get one last chance to talk directly to the jury in their *closing arguments*. Here, the lawyers can argue anything that is supported by the evidence. They ask the jury to use common sense. They ask the jury to believe, or disbelieve, various witnesses. They try to convince the jury to see the case in a certain way.

They jury leaves the courtroom to go to the jury deliberation room, guarded by a bailiff, so that no one can influence or have any effect on the jury. The jury discusses and debates the case in private. It's up to the jury to decide who told the truth, what actually happened, who said what to whom and when, and what Ann and Bob intended. In a California civil case, 9 of the 12 people must agree on a verdict. The jury will decide whether, for example, Ann proved the elements of fraud (i.e. elements 1-5 above). If yes, they decide how much money is fair compensation for Ann. If no, then they say so, and Ann loses the case. The jury indicates its decision on a written form called the *verdict form*. They come back into court when they are ready, and the written form is read out loud. And so the trial ends.

Trials are public—everyone has the right to watch. Everyone can see the process. Lawyers are never allowed to talk to the Judge (or the jury) out of the hearing of the other side, so the people involved in a case know exactly what the other side has said, and what arguments they made to the Judge and jury. Everyone has a opportunity to be heard, to object, to argue against the other side's evidence, to make his position known. Everyone has a right to fair and impartial jury, and the Judge has a strict obligation to protect that right. If the losing party thinks the Judge made a legal mistake, the party can appeal, and then an appellate court will review the law.

Thus, when in the end one side wins and the other side loses, people at least know what the evidence against them was, and they know they had a fair shot, a fair process. They are therefore willing to accept the final result, and move on with their lives. The dispute is over.

7.   Evidence: The Role of Judges & Juries

In a trial, both Judges and juries decide things, but they have very different roles. Judges handle the *legal* decisions, and juries handle the *factual* decisions. Let me provide a few examples. Assume the defendant (let's call him Don) is accused of stealing a car. A jury is selected, and the trial begins. There are a few basic factual issues: did Don take the car? Did he do so, knowing that it wasn't his? Who owned the car at the time? Did the theft take place about when the prosecutor says it did? The jury decides these issues.

There are many *legal* issue that can arise, too: if Don had a glass of wine before he took the car, is that enough for the Judge to instruct the jury on a defense of unconsciousness? If the owner testifies that he gave Don to permission to take the car, should the case be dismissed? The Judge decides these issues, too.

During trials, Judges decide many other legal issues as well, especially those concerning evidence. In every trial, the lawyers bring in evidence, such as the testimony of witnesses, documents, and sometimes objects such as a gun, or blood stains, or a piece of a car. The jury bases it decisions about the facts on this evidence. In a civil suit, such as one in which Alan is suing Beth for crashing into his car and breaking his leg, Alan might bring in his medical bills (to show how much he paid to fix the leg), the caved-in door of his car (to how hard the impact was), a map (to show where the accident took place), testimony from doctors, testimony from an accident reconstruction expert, and of course Alan's own testimony about how the accident took place. Beth will offer her own, perhaps conflicting evidence.

Now, the parties might *object* to some of this evidence, and those objections create legal issues that only the Judge can decide. If the Judge agrees with the objection that the evidence should not be admitted, the Judge *sustains* the objection. If the Judge disagrees with the objection, and thinks the evidence should come in, then the

—

Judge *overrules* the objection.

There are rules about what sorts of things (or testimony) can be "admitted" as evidence, and unless and until the Judge *admits* the evidence, the jury never sees it. Most of the rules of evidence have to do with basic reliability: the lawyer who wants to have something admitted has to show that there is *some* reason to trust the evidence. For example, the lawyer needs to show the map really is a map of the intersection of the accident: perhaps Alan will look at the map (or a photo of the scene), and say it looks correct. When it comes to medical bills, perhaps the doctor will say these are in fact the medical bills that relate to Alan's broken leg. Perhaps Alan or Beth will testify that the caved-in car door looks like it did right after the crash. In all of these cases, there is a basic amount of reliability to the evidence, and so the Judge will probably make the legal decision to *admit* the evidence. Once that happens, the jury gets to hear or see the evidence.

But that is not the end of the matter. The fact that evidence has been admitted does not mean the jury has to believe it, or rely on it. Alan might testify that the caved-in car door in the courtroom was just as it was after the accident, and as a result of the accident. So the Judge will admit the door. The jury will see it. But Beth might contradict Alan, and say that she actually hit Alan on the other side of the car; that the caved-in door was *not* the result of the accident. The Judge decides the legal issues of whether the door was admissible—but the jury decides the fact: whether the door really was broken as a result of the accident. A doctor's testimony that documents are in fact the bills he sent to Alan in connection with treating the broken leg might be enough to have the Judge make the legal decision to admit the bills—but Beth's lawyer might argue that the bills are outrageously high, or that the doctor is lying and the bills are really for something else—and the jury will in the end make the factual decision of whether the bills are reasonable and actually for the broken leg, and then whether Beth should pay Alan for the amount he spent on medical treatment.

Admissible evidence isn't necessarily true, and even if true, it might not be persuasive to the jury. The jury has the right to reject or accept any admissible evidence it gets.

Here's another example. Assume Beth's lawyer puts an accident reconstructionist on the stand. This guy is an expert: He used to work for the police department, and has been working for twenty years as an accident reconstruction expert. He looks at photos of the scene of an accident, measures tire skid marks, sees how much damage each car suffered, and then provides an opinion as to how the accident happened, or how fast a car was going at the time. The Judge, as a legal matter, might see enough about this fellow's background and experience to let him testify as an expert — the Judge may admit his testimony, in which case the jury will hear it. But the jury might not like the expert. The jury might think he's just making things up. Or the jury might think Alan's expert, who gives a different opinion, seems to be more reliable, makes more sense, has better credentials. The Judge may well admit both (conflicting) experts' testimony, and the jury then makes the fact determination of how the accident actually happened, perhaps by rejecting one of the expert's testimony.

The Judge does not decide who is telling the truth, or whether a document is persuasive. That's up to the jury. The Judge just decides whether there is enough for admission. The Judge would reject evidence — she would sustain the objection to the evidence — in situations such as, for example, when someone offers a print-out of a web page, but where no one testifies it really is from a certain web site. The Judge would stop an expert from testifying outside his area of expertise — for example, most doctors can't testify as accident reconstructionists. The Judge will sustain an objection to a question that calls for speculation ("How will the stock market do next year?").

Even lawyers get confused about the role of Judges and juries. In one case before me, a lawyer had his client testify that a document was a certain letter, which had been mailed to the other party. The lawyer then asked me to admit the letter into evidence. I asked the other party's lawyer if there was any objection (I always ask) — and he said yes, he objected, because *his* client was ready to testify that the letter had *never* been mailed, and so the letter was irrelevant.

But for me as a Judge, the testimony from one person that the letter was mailed is enough — I admitted the letter — and it was up to the jury to decide who was telling the truth.

Sometimes the legal issue of whether something can be admitted requires a hearing outside the presence of the jury, because it may be impossible to explore the legal issues without talking about the evidence in an obvious way. And sometimes, the Judge in those hearings does have to make decisions about who is telling the truth. Here's an example. There is some evidence which, although it looks relevant and reliable, still can not be admitted. The attorney-client communication privilege might have that effect. What lawyers and clients say to each other is private, and usually cannot be admitted in court (although it might be *very* interesting to hear!). That's just the law. So, assume that Alan is on the stand answering questions, and he's asked whether he ever spoke about the accident with Roger, a friend who happens to be a lawyer. Alan (or his lawyer) now objects, citing the attorney-client privilege — conversations between Alan and Roger cannot be admitted, Alan says. But there's an issue here-- *was* Alan really talking to Roger as a *friend*, or as an *attorney*? It makes a difference, and the Judge will have to decide that factual issue before he can decide whether the attorney-client privilege objection is a good one or not. The Judge might decide to believe (or not believe) Roger and Alan if they testify on the subject. All this will take place outside the presence of the jury.

But recall, even if the Judge admits the evidence, it is the jury that ultimately decides what to do with the evidence- whether to rely on it, whether it's accurate, whether it is outweighed by other, conflicting evidence. The jury has the final say.

8.   Sentencing

At the end of a criminal trial, the jury may find the defendant guilty, or not guilty. Sometimes the jury of twelve people cannot agree, in which case the Judge declares a *mistrial* and the case has to be re-tried. If the defendant is found not guilty, the case is over and the defendant walks out of the courthouse—assuming there are no remaining charges.

But if the defendant is found guilty, the Judge must set a date for sentencing. Sometimes, especially with relatively minor crimes, the sentencing can take place almost immediately. In other cases, it may be important to allow the defendant, and the prosecutor, time to investigate and prepare papers for the Judge on the factors that may influence the sentence.

At sentencing Judges are often called on to make very difficult choices, trying at the same time to protect the public and to account for the particular circumstances of the defendant's conditions. (More on those factors below.)

How much discretion does a Judge have? The basic limits on sentencing are set by the Legislature—the law itself states the maximum sentence. (Most of those laws are in the Penal Code.) For an example, let us take a relatively simple misdemeanor, driving while under the influence of a drug or alcohol—as we say, a "DUI." A "misdemeanor" is punishable by up to a year in custody; a "felony" is more serious, punishable by some term in custody for more than one year. In a misdemeanor DUI, the Judge can send the defendant to jail for up to a year, plus impose a series of fees, fines, and penalties which can add up to many thousands of dollars. But the court can also *suspend* the imposition of a sentence, impose the fines, and put the defendant on probation for, say, three years: If the defendant adheres to the conditions of probation—conditions such as committing no more crimes, and attending classes on drugs and driving—then he will have, in effect, completed his sentence. Or the Judge could do some of both, for example, send the defendant to jail for a shorter period, such as two months, plus three years of probation. If the defendant violates the terms of his probation, then the Judge can (after a hearing) "revoke" the probation and send the defendant to jail for any period up to a total of a year. A Judge can also revoke probation and then put the defendant back on probation, perhaps with new conditions.

For felonies, it is more difficult to map out how much room the Judge has in sentencing. Generally, for a first offense, the Judge still can choose between prison time and probation, or a mixture of both. For a first felony offense, in calculating prison time the Judge usually must choose one of three terms of imprisonment—we call this the "triad." For example, the Legislature might make a crime punishable by a triad of sixteen months, or two years, or three years in prison. The Judge will decide which of the three terms to use depending on many *mitigating* or *aggravating* factors. That period of incarceration might then be increased because of the particular way the crime was committed; for example, the Judge might add more time because a weapon was used, or a victim was injured, or the crimes showed very high sophistication.

Here is an example of a felony sentencing. Suppose a public official is convicted of bribery. The triad is set by the Legislature as two, three or four years. Penal Code § 68. The Judge might suspend the imposition of sentence, and put the defendant on probation. (For some crimes, the Judge is barred by law from allowing probation.) Or if the Judge thinks prison time is appropriate, she must decide, based on the circumstances, which term of the triad (2, 3 or 4 years) to use. Perhaps the defendant used a weapon in getting the bribe— that might increase the sentence upwards. California Rules of Court (CRC) 4.421. Perhaps the defendant took the bribe only after a lot of pressure, or others were actually more culpable, or he needed the money to pay for his spouse's cancer treatment bills—perhaps those factors might drive the sentence downwards. CRC 4.423.

When the defendant has *previously* been convicted of a serious or violent felony, the Judge has to follow rules commonly known as the "three strikes" law. A "strike" is a prior conviction of a certain kind of felony; in fact, the rules cover what we might call "two strikes" as well as three strikes. If the current case is his second felony — if this is his second strike — then the Judge may have to double the sentence she would otherwise impose. If this is his third strike — that is, if the defendant was previously convicted of *two* serious or violent felonies — then the Judge may have to sentence the defendant to state prison for <u>at least</u> 25 years, up to life, in prison.

The analysis of what *type* of felonies count as "strikes" can be difficult. There are also very complex formulas Judges have to deal with when a defendant is convicted of *multiple* counts, each with a different possible sentence, for example, when he is convicted of robbery, <u>and</u> extortion, <u>and</u> kidnapping, all arising out of one series of facts. But in most cases, whether the Judge is deciding between some jail time and probation, or which of the three levels in a triad to use, the Judge has some flexibility, and is called on to exercise his or her discretion based on a series of various factors.

Most of the factors that go into the sentencing decision fall into one of two areas: factors directly about the defendant, and factors affecting the public. These factors stem from the purposes of sentencing: protecting society, punishment, deterrence of the defendant and others by showing the result of committing crime; preventing the defendant from committing new crimes during the period of incarceration, obtaining victim restitution, and creating uniform sentences.

Factors affecting sentencing point in different directions. This is an uncomfortable truth that is actually recognized by the California Rules of Court (CRC) that apply to sentencing. CRC 4.410(b). Examples of factors directly about the defendant are his prior criminal record, or lack of one; whether he appears to be violent, whether he was on probation when arrested for the present crime, his performance on prior probations, encouraging the defendant to be law abiding in the future; whether he admitted guilt early on in the proceedings; whether the defendant tried to pay the victim back; and so on. Factors concerning the public also include whether or not the defendant is dangerous; whether or not the crime involved a weapon; whether someone was hurt; if the defendant induced others to join him in the crime; whether a large amount of money was involved; how sophisticated the crime appeared; and whether the crime was a "hate crime," i.e., directed to a victim because of the victim's race, gender, sexual orientation, and so on. Penal Code § 422.55, CRC 4.427.

Sentencing is not easy. Sometimes the Judge has very few real choices, but often the Judge has to consider a wide variety of factors: following the various instructions and policies of the Legislature, accounting for the harm done to the victims, tailoring the sentence to the specific defendant in court, and also trying to predict and account for future risk to the public.

*

Resources relating to this article

California Rules of Court: http://www.courts.ca.gov/rules.htm
California Penal Code: http://www.leginfo.ca.gov/cgi-bin/calawquery?codesection=pen
A free way to find court decisions: http://scholar.google.com/

Note: recent changes in the law determine whether a defendant convicted of a felony will serve time in state prison or a local county jail. These changes are ignored in this essay.

9. Alternative Dispute Resolution

Some of us may think of the courtroom as the only place where legal disagreements can be resolved. But people involved in lawsuits—or people who believe they are *about* to be involved in a lawsuit—have some other options. They can agree on alternative procedures, outside of the courtroom, to resolve their differences. There are many ways to do this. We describe these as types of *alternative dispute resolution* (ADR).

People can decide to sue someone else for a variety of reasons, usually because they feel they have been damaged by another person. A person seeking to bring a suit (we call this a plaintiff) might have been injured in a car accident, and wants to sue the other driver (who would be the defendant). Two people or two companies engaged in a business venture might sue each other if the business goes bad and they each blame the other. Someone might sue an employer, or employee, if they think the employment contract was breached; for example the employee might sue for unpaid wages, or an employer might sue if it thought an employee stole software from the workplace. Landlords and tenants sue each other; and the list goes on. In all of these cases, the plaintiff and the defendant (the "parties") can simply allow the law to take its course and have the case resolved by a court, perhaps through the use of a jury trial. But in all these cases, the parties might, instead, agree to some sort of ADR.

There are two basic types of ADR. One type tries to help the parties reach an agreement. The other imposes a result on the parties, very much like a court judgment is imposed on the parties. I discuss these two types in order.

Mediation and Settlement. Most cases actually do not end up being resolved by a Judge or a jury; instead, the parties reach a voluntary agreement—they *settle* the case. Even in hard fought cases, where passions run high and each side is utterly convinced it is absolutely right and the other is as wrong as wrong can be—even

---

in these cases, the odds are very high—about 80%--that the case filed in court will eventually settle. There comes a point in these cases where the parties realize that instead of paying the costs of litigation and running the risk of a bad decision, they can instead compromise, stop the litigation, and get perhaps some, if not all, of what they want. A plaintiff can get some of the money he thinks he is owed; a settling defendant may pay a fraction of what he might have to pay after a court judgment.

So how do cases settle? First, it's important to note that people can enter into settlement negotiations before anything is ever filed in court. Many disputes which settle never see the inside of a courtroom at all. The lawyers might be wise, and after speaking with the clients, might start settlement discussions. Or the parties go to a professional mediator and have a mediation session. In a mediation--a form of settlement conference-- the mediator speaks with both sides. He often speaks privately and separately with the parties to get an idea of what the dispute is really about and what the parties really need. Then he uses his skills to bring the parties together, perhaps by talking about the strengths and weaknesses of each person's case. Eventually, the mediator may be able to have both sides reach a voluntary agreement.

Many lawyers and retired Judges are experts at mediation (although anyone can be a mediator—one need not have been a lawyer). Many fulltime Judges, too, are skilled at conducting settlement conferences. So even after a case has started in the courts, the Judge might order the parties to a settlement conference with her (or some other Judge), or might encourage the parties to go outside the courthouse and try a session with a professional mediator. Many lawyers also volunteer their time to act as mediators. Sometimes a mediator will not succeed in resolving the case there and then, but he does get the parties to think about various options, and the lawyers involved in the case thereafter might get together to come up with a settlement plan for their clients. At every stage of the litigation good lawyers are always thinking about how a reasonable settlement might be achieved. Indeed, some cases settle after the trial has started, and some settle when they are on appeal, years after the case started in the trial court.

There's another variant of settlement called "early neutral evaluation" or ENE. Here, the parties get together with a neutral person, often a lawyer who has volunteered to help. As the name suggests, ENE takes places early, before the parties have spent a lot of money. The idea is to provide a "reality check" to the parties on the strengths of their case, and to avoid lengthy, expensive litigation when it's fairly clear that one side or the other does not have a good case. The ENE conference also gets the parties thinking about settlement generally, and can set the stage for a later settlement conference, allowing the case to resolve then.

Arbitration. The other type of ADR is arbitration. Here, the parties have *not* agreed on a result, they have *not* resolved their differences. But they have agreed on one thing—the *procedure* by which their dispute will be resolved. They have agreed that instead of the courts, instead of a Judge and/or jury, they will use an arbitrator to decide the case. Just as with mediators, many arbitrators are professionals, perhaps lawyers or retired Judges. When they decide a case, it's just as if a Judge decided it. And if the losing side refuses to abide by the arbitrator's judgment, then the winning side can go to court to force the losing side to do what it was supposed to do— Judges usually do enforce the decisions of arbitrators.

Why would parties give up their right to have a trial in court, and instead opt for an arbitration? There are a number of reasons. First, arbitration is private. Instead of talking in a public courtroom about issues which might be embarrassing, or discussing in public sensitive matters such as income, tax returns, or other issues which a party might think private, arbitrations are conducted in offices; and the public and the press can be excluded. Secondly, the arbitration agreement might include provisions which reduce the time and cost of litigation. They might agree to limited pre-trial preparation, such as being able to ask each for a limited number of documents, or to pose only a few pre-trial inquiries to the other side. Some people think that, for this and other reasons, arbitrations are less costly and time-consuming than litigation in court. Sometimes that is true, and sometimes it is not. It depends very much on which arbitrator is selected.

Parties might agree to arbitration before or after the lawsuit is started in court; typically, the arbitration requirement is part of a pre-existing contract between the parties. For example, there may be an arbitration requirement in your contract with your employer; there may be one in your agreement with your telecommunications provider (cell phone, cable), or in the agreement you sign when renting a car or a vacation apartment, or in the contract signed with the cruise line when you booked a cruise. In all of these cases the arbitration clause in your contract might force you to resolve your dispute through arbitration, and make it impossible to have a court handle the matter.

Even when there are arbitration clauses, there are two situations where Judges have a role. First, there may be a disagreement on whether or not, in the first place, there *is* an arbitration clause that applies. A Judge may need to decide if certain language in the contract really is an agreement to go to arbitration; the Judge may decide that even if the clause exists, it does not apply because the *entire* contract which contains the clause is invalid for some reason. Sometimes, even when the clause is valid and obviously requires arbitration, a Judge decides that the *particular* dispute at issue is not covered by the clause. For example a clause might require arbitration of every "employment related" dispute between an employer and an employee — and the present dispute is not, *exactly*, about "employment" issues, but has to do with e.g., the alleged theft of software. Sometimes Judges make these decisions; sometimes the arbitrator himself decides whether there is a valid arbitration clause.

Judges also get involved in arbitration when the winning side wants to *enforce* the arbitrator's award, or the losing side wants to *vacate* the award. So, after the arbitration is completed, the case may return to court. The Judge will usually enforce the award, but sometimes the Judge has to vacate it. For example, the court might vacate if the arbitrator had decided he should hear the case, but in fact the arbitration clause did not cover the dispute; or the court might vacate if the arbitrator did not allow one side to even put on its case, or was entirely arbitrary and completely unfair, or was paid a bribe by one side. As I suggest, it is rare that an arbitration award is vacated, because courts want to honor and respect the agreements people make to have arbitrations.

People who provide ADR services can be very valuable. Some provide limited services for free, such as those helping with ENE; some are very expensive, costing many, many thousands of dollars a day, but in the end they may save the parties a lot of time and money. Judges of course do not charge for settlement conferences they supervise. When compared to the possible costs and uncertainty of continued litigation, ADR is often a wise course.

10. Appeals

You got a traffic ticket. And you want to appeal. You're furious
that the trial Judge went along with the story told by the police
officer — your version was so much more credible, and anyway, you
had a witness who confirmed you were telling the truth! Yet the
Judge still tagged you with a fine. Appellate courts are supposed to
fix such injustices, aren't they?

They are not.

Appellate courts and trial courts have very different roles (with one
exception I'll get to, concerning Small Claims). And indeed, the
Supreme Court has a different role from that of other appellate
courts.

First, a brief reminder of the structure of our courts. Recall that the
federal government has its court system for federal cases, and each
state has a court system for cases arising under state law. In each of
these systems, we begin with the trial courts: in California these are
known as the Superior Court. Appeals go to the Court of Appeal.
From there, a losing party can ask the California Supreme Court to
take the case.

There are fifty-eight Superior Courts in this state, one for each
county. Those courts have from two to many hundreds of Judges.
There are six Courts of Appeal responsible for different areas of the
state; and one Supreme Court.

(Actually, it's a little more complicated than that, because in
California we have two different tracks to appeal cases. I have just
described the track that criminal felony cases take (a felony is a
crime punishable by more than a year in state prison), as well as

civil lawsuits where the amount of money at stake is more than $25,000. But if the case is not a felony (i.e. it's a misdemeanor, punishable by up to a year in jail, or an infraction, only punishable by a fine, like a traffic ticket), or if the case is a civil suit worth less than $25,000, the appeal from the Superior Court is to a court known as the *Appellate Division*. But the sequence is almost the same, and the same sort of rules apply whether the appeal is to the Court of Appeal or to the Appellate Division.)

A word, first, about the difference between a legal issue and a factual issue. This will help explain what different kinds of Judges do.

Often, people in a lawsuit disagree about what happened in the past. In a traffic accident case, Ann says the light was red, Bob says it was green. In a contract case, Bob says Ann promised to sell her cat; Ann swears she never made such a promise. These are disputes about facts: *about what happened*. Some disputes are about the law; these are *legal* disputes. Ann might argue that it doesn't matter what color the light was, because under the law Bob had to stop *anyway* when he saw Ann's car; or in the contract case Ann might argue that under the law it doesn't matter if she agreed to sell a cat, because it's illegal to sell cats (of course, I am not saying that *is* the law).

This difference between fact issue and legal issues is important to understanding the difference between the jobs of trial Judges and appellate Judges.

As I suggested, trial Judges and appellate Judges do not do the same thing. A trial Judge deciding a traffic ticket is entitled to believe whomever she wants. She can believe one witness instead of three other people who say something else. She's looking at body language, looking at the witnesses as they testify. She decides who is telling the truth. She decides what happened. An appellate Judge can't do that. Appellate Judges have no idea who is telling the truth. If a trial Judge decides to believe a drug addicted convicted murderer, and reject the word of a respected member of the community such as the Mayor — well, the Judge is entitled to do so. Appellate Judges usually never tamper with the *factual findings* of the trial Judge.

There are two other sorts of decisions trial Judges make. Appellate courts might reverse some of those.

First, trial Judges decide *legal* issues: they decide what the law is. I provided some examples of legal issues before. A few more examples: the trial Judge might decide that the law requires a certain type of lawsuit (say, breach of an agreement) to be brought to court within 4 years of the breach—and so, if more than 4 years went by, the Judge would dismiss the case. Or she might decide that certain evidence cannot be admitted at trial (say, a photograph, or a written document). Or a Judge might decide that there's no such thing as a certain kind of legal claim (for example, she might decide that you just *can't* sue your neighbor for laughing at your car's weird paint scheme.) Those sorts of legal determinations can be reviewed by the appellate courts; and if the decision of the trial Judge was wrong, then the appellate court might reverse the decision and send the case back for another trial, or some other proceeding.

(But it is important to recall that, to reverse, the trial Judge's wrong decision has to have a made a *difference to the outcome.* So, for example, if the Judge was wrong to exclude a photograph from a trial, but admitting it would have made no difference to the result, then the appellate court will not reverse. This is a rule called "harmless error." No harm, no foul.)

The third kind of decision trial Judges make is, in a way, between the two types I've discussed—these are *discretionary* decisions, where the trial Judge has room to decide an issue either way. A lot of these decisions are relatively trivial, and you won't be surprised to learn that appellate courts usually do not reverse trial Judges on their discretionary decisions. Discretionary decisions range from everything from where lawyers stand in a courtroom, how much time they can have to ask questions, and which days will be set aside for trial, to more important issues such as letting in evidence when, although admissible, it might possibly prejudice the other party. For example, Judges use their discretion in deciding whether the jury will see gruesome photos of a murder scene — the photos are probably relevant and admissible, but they might have an *emotional* impact on the jury that might not be fair to the person accused of the crime. Another example: when lawyers fail to follow the rules (such as filing papers late, or not at all), Judges use their discretion in deciding whether to punish a lawyer with fines, or to refuse to read the late paper. Judges also use their discretion in sentencing after a criminal trial.

Appellate courts don't like to reverse Judges for these sorts of discretionary rulings — although, if the ruling is really bizarre and arbitrary, or simply had no basis at all (i.e. the papers weren't late at all!), the appellate courts will then reverse. And if a Judge sentences a criminal defendant to ten years in prison, and the law only allows one year, that's not a discretionary ruling — that's legal error. And the Court of Appeal will reverse.

Again, the theory here is that the trial Judge is the person who really knows what's happening, what is needed to keep cases moving fairly and rapidly, and how the jury is likely to react. Appellate Judges don't see the trial, or the witnesses, or the jury. All they have is the stone cold record — the transcript of the trial, and the papers filed by the lawyers — and they see this perhaps a year or more after the trial.

So, trial and appellate Judges have very different roles; except in one sort of case, which is termed *Small Claims*. Small Claims court is available for people who want to sue someone for up to $7500. There are no lawyers at trial, and the trial is very fast and efficient. It's a good way for people to ask the courts to resolve many disputes. If the person who started the suit — the plaintiff — loses in Small Claims, the case is over. There's no appeal. But if the person *defending* the case (the defendant) loses, he does have a right to appeal: he gets a new trial in front a different Judge, and this time, lawyers can be present. This is an exception to the usual course — because here the second trial really *is* a new start — no one cares what the first Judge did. This kind of 'appeal' is called a trial *de novo*: a new proceeding.

———

Once an appellate court has decided an appeal, that's usually the end of it: the trial decision gets affirmed; or reversed, or gets reversed and *remanded*, which means the case goes back to the trial court for more proceedings (perhaps another trial). Whatever the appellate courts does, that's usually the end of the matter. It's very difficult to get the decision of the appellate court itself reversed — the only court that can do that is the Supreme Court. And while we usually have a "right of appeal" to the appellate court, there is *no right* to go the Supreme Court (the only exceptions are death penalty cases, which are automatically appealed to the Supreme Court).

The Supreme Court *chooses* which cases it will hear. It usually never takes a case just because it thinks the lower appellate court was wrong; and it sometimes takes cases even when it appears the appellate court was *right*. The Supreme Court takes only about 100 case a year (compared to the eight million cases filed every year in the trial courts), and does so only when there are very important, state-wide issues, or when different courts of appeal have decided a legal issue in opposite ways. The intermediate courts of appeal are there to correct legal errors for the particular parties in that case. But the Supreme Court does not have that role: it settles important statewide issues, issues that affect a lot of people.

The different types of Judges on our courts systems have very different jobs, and look at different issues: it's a division of labor. Arguments that may be effective with a trial Judge may make no difference to an appellate Judge. Together, all the courts work to make sure that people and companies get fair hearings, that significant mistakes are corrected, and that there is consistency of law across the entire state.

11.   The Juvenile Delinquency System, Simply Described

By Hon. Patrick Mahoney

The juvenile delinquency system is set up to address the needs of youth who get in trouble with the law. The system is based on providing services to youth to address their needs. The goal is to ensure that they do not return and over 75% of those entering the system never return.

Those who do enter the system generally are truant from school and/or are having behavior problems when in school; there is instability in their home life due to a lack of parenting skills, absent parents, substance abuse or mental health needs; and more often than not the family is poor. These factors cause youth to make bad decisions and those decisions cause them to be in the juvenile justice system.

The legal process tracks the adult system but employs different language. A young person may receive a citation, for example using marijuana, or may be arrested for committing a serious crime, such as a violent assault upon another. In either event, the youth appears before a Judge.

If the youth is detained in juvenile hall before the hearing, the first hearing is referred to as a detention hearing. The youth is entitled to a lawyer and to have his or her parents present. The charges are explained as are the youth's right to a trial. The first issue is whether the person is to be detained, meaning he or she must remain in juvenile hall. The analysis looks at public safety, the needs of the youth, and the stability in the home. If the youth is detained, the person is entitled to an expedited hearing (within 15 court days) to determine if the charges can be proved beyond a reasonable doubt, the highest standard of proof.

If the youth is not detained but receives a citation to appear, the first hearing is referred to a jurisdictional hearing (J-1) to explain the charges, the youth's rights and to set the matter for a further hearing.

At every hearing, the youth's parents are notified and requested to be present. A probation officer is assigned to the case and is responsible for gathering information about the youth, the family, schooling, and needs so that a recommendation can be made to the court as to the best strategy to address the needs of the youth that have influenced the commission of the crime.

The next hearing is generally a pre trial conference to determine if the case needs to have a trial or whether it can be resolved by the youth's engaging in a diversion program or admitting to the charge(s). Diversion programs provide services to the youth and often the family and may include substance abuse counseling, therapy and participation in a youth oriented program. In every case, the youth is obligated to attend school and to refrain from getting into any further trouble. If the youth does what is required, the charges are dismissed and the file is sealed.

If the case proceeds to trial, the prosecutor must prove that one or more of the crimes charged was committed beyond a reasonable doubt. The trial is similar to an adult trial except there is no jury. Witnesses testify and are cross examined by the attorney for the youth; the youth may but is not required to testify; and witnesses may be called by the defense. The rules of evidence determine what facts the Judge considers. At the end of the trial, the lawyers argue their side of the case to the Judge. After considering the evidence, the Judge decides whether a crime has been committed. If no, the case is dismissed. If yes, the Judge sets the case for a disposition hearing; this is the equivalent to a sentencing hearing in the adult system.

The disposition hearing determines what the best plan is to address the youth's long term needs. If this is a first offense, it is customary for the youth to stay at home and be ordered to participate in services, such as substance abuse counseling, drug testing, therapy and community service. A nightly curfew is put in place, the youth may not possess weapons of any kind and must always attend school. The youth is assigned a probation officer to ensure that the services are available and the youth participates. Periodically, the youth's performance is reviewed and if all is well after one year, the case is dismissed.

If the case involves a very serious crime and or the youth has committed multiple offenses, he or she may be removed from the home and sent to a group home, a more restrictive county ranch program or even a locked facility for the most serious crimes. In these programs, there is more intensive oversight of the youth because his/her needs could not be addressed at home.

Those who work in the juvenile justice system – the Judges, the prosecutors, the defense lawyers, the probation officers, the educators and mental health professionals – are always looking for ways to make the system better. There are regular meetings to address needs, statewide conferences to share information, and research to enhance the ability of the providers to meet the needs of youth.

Over the years, collaborative courts have become increasingly common to address specific needs. For example, there may be a Family Violence Court that addresses violence in the home and in dating relationships; a Behavioral Health Court to address the needs of youth with significant mental health needs; a School Court that oversees a high school program designed for at risk youth; and a Re-entry court to ensure that youth who have been placed out of home are able to effectively return home. In these courts, the goal of the participants is to come to a common plan on what is in the youth's best interest given the particular facts of the case. Every effort is made to avoid contested hearings and to implement a service plan that works. Youth who are in these courts tend to have specialized needs and the focus is on addressing the needs so that their behavior is changed.

In the final analysis, the juvenile justice system is not based on punishment; it is based on hope and helping those who come into the system.

12. What Happens In Family Court?

By Hon. Rebecca L. Wightman and Hon. Monica F. Wiley

Often when one thinks of family court, the word "divorce" comes to mind. Family courts, however, deal with various matters relating to a family, including disputes over property and children. Some California courts have an entire division, called a "Unified Family Court," where different courtrooms hear cases involving children and families, including cases involving juvenile crimes (Juvenile Delinquency), child abuse or neglect (Juvenile Dependency), domestic violence, custody, visitation, child support, adoptions and guardianships (where a non-parent seeks to be a child's guardian).

Most family courts handle disputes involving: (1) marriage or a domestic partner relationship, (2) divisions of property when there's a breakup of a marriage (partnership), and (3) children, including support, custody and visitation issues.

Family courts also handle requests concerning minors (someone under 18 years old), such as a minor's request for emancipation (to be free from parental control), and can refer people to services such as counseling, mediation, or parenting classes.

DIVORCE: ENDING A MARRIAGE OR REGISTERED DOMESTIC PARTNERSHIP

In California, a marriage or registered domestic partnership relationship can be ended by divorce, legal separation (where the parties stay married, but are legally separated), or annulment. This allows them to get court orders dividing their property, or support orders (where one person helps financially support another). The filing of a "Petition for Dissolution" starts the divorce process. California is a "no fault" divorce state, which means that whoever is asking for the divorce doesn't have to prove that anyone did anything wrong. One spouse (partner) simply has to state that the couple cannot get along. Legally, this is called "irreconcilable differences." If the other person doesn't want to get divorced, they cannot stop the process. If someone ignores the legal papers received requesting a divorce, the other person can get a "default" judgment and the divorce will happen.

If the marriage or partnership was not "valid" to begin with, meaning the legal requirements for getting married did not exist at the time (such as not being old enough to consent to marriage, still being married to someone else, getting married through fraud [deception] or under duress) then the marriage can be ended by a judgment of "Nullity" (an "annulment").

The main issues that commonly arise in a divorce, separation or annulment are:
- Financial issues – including "division of property" and "support" issues (spousal and/or child support);
- "Custody and Visitation" or parenting issues – for children from the relationship.

We discuss these topics below.

FAMILY COURT: FINANCIAL ISSUES

Division of Property: When parties separate or get divorced, a court must decide how to divide their property. Some examples of property that may need to be divided are: houses, cars, furniture, bank accounts, jewelry, and even pensions (money normally paid upon retirement). A court must also determine how to divide any debts (money owed) the parties have. Who gets what property depends largely on *when* the property was acquired. Property acquired *before* the marriage or domestic partnership, is called "separate" property, and belongs to the person who originally got it. Property acquired *during* the marriage, is called "community" property. Community property belongs equally to the parties, and if the parties cannot agree on how to divide everything, courts have the authority to order the property be sold and the proceeds divided between them.

Support Orders: Support orders involve court decisions on *how much should be paid* for spousal or child support (if there are children) and *how long* the support must be paid.

"Spousal support" is money paid by one spouse (partner) to another. The purpose of this order is to help the spouse (partner) getting the support to become self-sufficient (able to pay his or her own bills) within a reasonable period of time. A spousal support order made while the divorce case is pending is a "*temporary*" order. Spousal support that extends *after* the case is over (after the divorce becomes final) is called "*permanent*" or long term spousal (partner) support.

There is no fixed formula to determine the duration of a "permanent" spousal support order. Courts look at the length of the marriage (partnership). Generally, a "reasonable period of time" may be one-half the length of the marriage, but the Judge can decide differently, depending on the facts. One important exception is when a marriage (partnership) is "long term" – generally 10 years or more – in which case the Judge may not initially set any end date to the spousal support.

The Judge considers many factors in setting the amount of spousal or partner support, including:
- Length of the marriage (or domestic partnership)
- Age, health, employment skills
- Income of each person, and what each one needs to maintain the "standard of living" established during the marriage (partnership)
- Amount of debts (obligations) and assets (property, stocks, etc.)

After a final spousal support amount is set, a change can be requested if a significant event occurs. For example, the person receiving support may no longer need it, or the person paying support may lose his job (and now is unable to pay); or maybe the person getting support isn't really trying to become self-supporting. A spousal support order can end on the date set by court order, or when one of the spouses (partner) dies, or when the person getting the support remarries or registers a new domestic partnership.

"Child support" is the amount of money a person must pay to help with a child's living expenses. Each parent is equally responsible for contributing to the financial needs of his or her children. A parent cannot refuse to let the other parent see the child just because child support isn't being paid. Nor can a parent refuse to pay child support if the other parent doesn't allow visitation.

One's status as a parent ("parentage") must be established before a court can make a child support order. Generally, this can be done through a voluntary "Declaration of Paternity" (a written statement parents usually sign at the hospital when the child is born), by genetic testing, or by a court determination.

The *amount* of child support is determined by using a statewide guideline. If the parents don't reach an agreement, the Judge will set the amount based upon the guideline. Different financial information goes into the calculation, but it mainly includes:

- How much each parent earns, and
- Amount of time each parent spends with the child.

Generally, the more time a parent spends with their child, the lower the support amount ordered, in order to encourage a parent's participation in the child's life. In addition to child support, the court may require parents to share in childcare or educational expenses.

Once set by court order, child support continues until it is changed or the order expires. A parent must show a "substantial change in circumstance" has occurred to change the amount. Some examples include: losing a job, having more children, or getting injured on the job. Child support orders expire when a child turns 18 (unless still in high school full time, then orders end upon graduation or 19, whichever occurs first). If a child continues to be disabled beyond emancipation, the responsibility to pay child support can continue indefinitely.

FAMILY COURT: CUSTODY AND VISITATION ISSUES

Any parent (regardless of marital status) can go to family court to resolve disputes regarding their children. "Custody" disputes involve *who* gets to make the major decisions concerning a child, and *where* a child lives. "Visitation" disputes involve what type of visitation schedule is appropriate.

There are two types of custody: legal and physical. "Legal custody" means *who gets to make major or important decisions* about a child's heath, education or welfare. These decisions include things like where to live, what school to attend, health care and travel decisions. A court can order *"joint"* legal custody – where both parents have equal decision-making authority, or *"sole"* legal custody – where only one parent makes these decisions. "Physical custody" refers to *whom the child lives with*. A *"joint"* physical custody order means the child may live with both parents at different times (not necessarily an equal amount of time). A *"sole"* physical custody order means the child lives with one parent and may visit the other.

Parents should try to agree on a plan for decision-making (outlining legal and physical custody arrangements), and the visitation schedule. Parents must consider the basic needs of their children (housing, health and medical issues), the ages, personalities, experiences and abilities of their children, holiday schedules, and other issues.

When parents don't agree, the court will make the custody decision based upon what is in the *best interest of the child* (not necessarily what plan either parent requests). The court will consider many of the factors mentioned earlier, including the child's age and health, emotional ties to each parent, home life, school and community, and the ability of a parent to care for the child. The court must also consider any history of family violence or drug or alcohol abuse by a parent.

There are many types of custody and visitation arrangements possible. If the parents live far apart, an order may include regular phone calls, holidays and summer breaks staying with the other parent. Orders can also be made for "reasonable visitation" which is open-ended, allowing parents to make their own arrangements not tied to any schedule. If there are safety concerns, "supervised visitation" can be ordered where visits occur with a relative or neutral person present at a specific location. A court can also order *no* visitation if it is not in the child's best interest to allow contact (i.e., visits may be emotionally or physically harmful to a child).

Courts do not automatically give custody to the mother or father, and cannot deny custody or visitation rights just because someone never married, has a physical disability, or different religious belief or sexual orientation.

*

Resources:

Family Law Facilitator [FLF]: Every county has an FLF office run by the court that provides free help to individuals who don't have an attorney. They help fill out family law forms, explain procedures on how to get/change child support orders, and how courts makes child support decisions.

Department of Child Support Services [DCSS]: State agency that oversees delivery of child support services in California. Every county has a Local Child Support Agency **[LCSA]** that helps people establish parentage, child support orders, collect orders, and get medical insurance orders. They also help locate parents. They do **not** provide divorce, custody or visitation services.

www.childsup.ca.gov Department of Child Support Services

www.sfgov.org/dcss   SF Department of Child Support
Services [LCSA]

www.courts.ca.gov   California Courts website (click Self-Help)

Appendix

State Courts

Source: http://www.courts.ca.gov/8753.htm

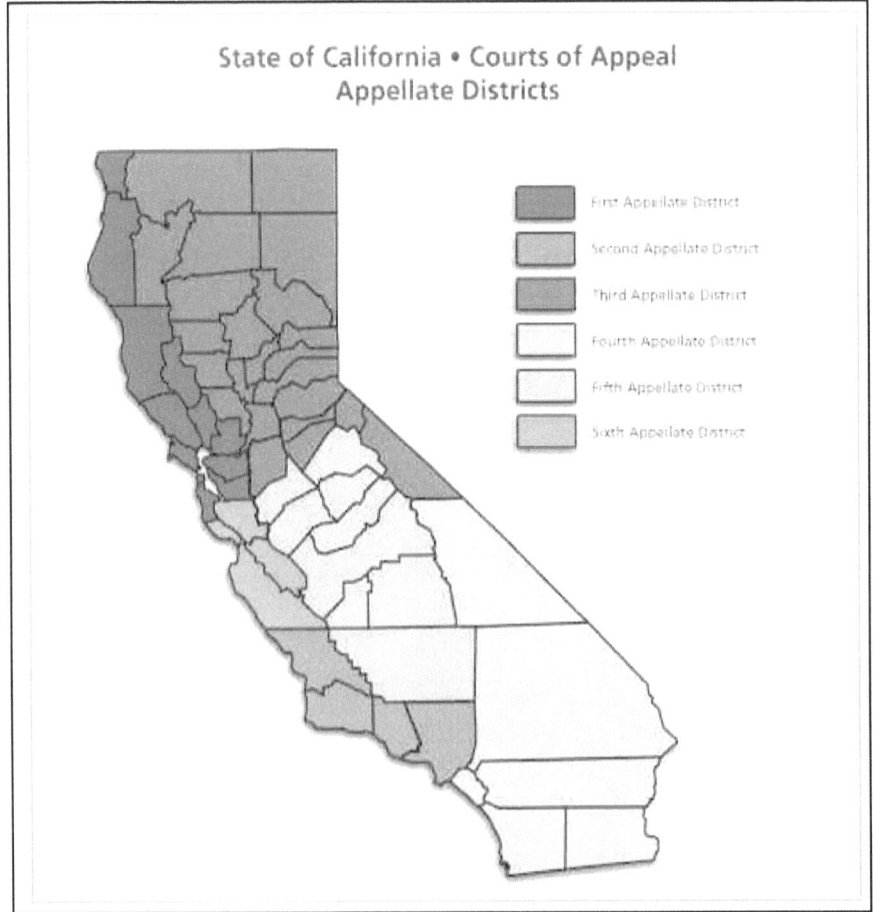

State of California • Courts of Appeal
Appellate Districts

First Appellate District
Second Appellate District
Third Appellate District
Fourth Appellate District
Fifth Appellate District
Sixth Appellate District

This shows the counties grouped by Appellate Districts. For example, appeals from the Superior (trial) courts in the northwestern part of the state including the Bay Area go to the First Appellate District; appeals from the southern counties (such as San Diego) go to the Fourth Appellate District; and so on.

Appendix
Federal Courts

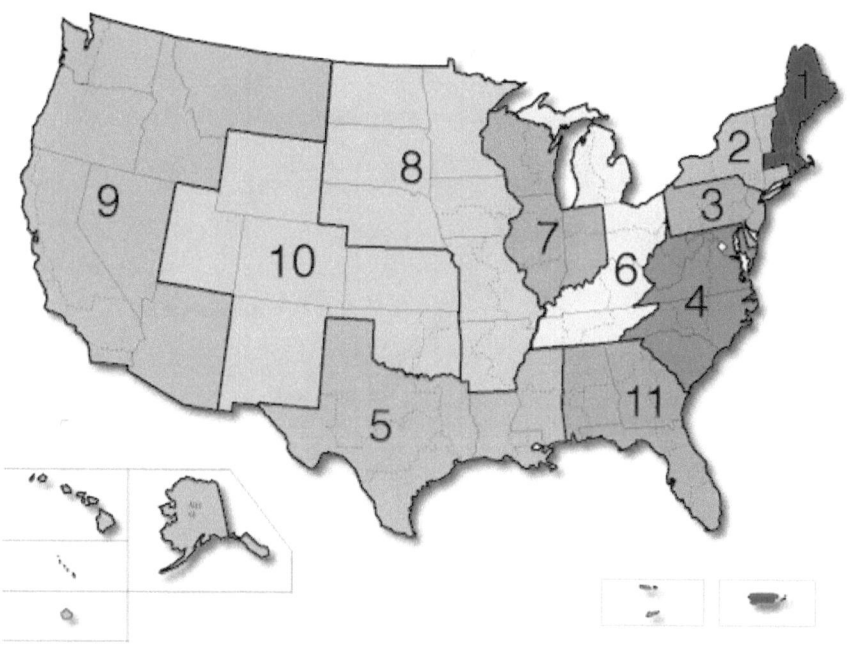

The United States is divided into various federal Circuits, each of which usually include a number of states. California is in the Ninth Circuit, along with Washington, Oregon, Hawaii, and other western states. A federal Court of Appeals is in charge of each Circuit, so that we have for example the Ninth Circuit Court of Appeals for the far western states including California, the First Circuit Court of Appeals for states in the north-east, and so on.

Northern District of California
Eastern District of California
Central District of California
Southern District of California

Within each of the states, we have various federal districts. Some states, such as Colorado, Nevada, Idaho, Montana and others, are a single district. California has a lot of people, and is composed of four districts: the Northern, Southern, Eastern and Central Districts. There are federal trial courthouses in each of these districts, and appeals from all federal trial courts in California go the Court of Appeals for the Ninth Circuit, which is headquartered in San Francisco. On the prior page, as well as the areas shown here, one can see the dotted lines within California which show these district lines.

www.ingramcontent.com/pod-product-compliance
Lightning Source LLC
Chambersburg PA
CBHW021831170526
45157CB00007B/2761